T0318326

Change and Execute

Change and Execute

How to Transform and Design Your Business for Sustained Success

Kevin E. Phillips

Routledge
Taylor & Francis Group

A PRODUCTIVITY PRESS BOOK

First published 2021
by Routledge
600 Broken Sound Parkway #300, Boca Raton FL, 33487

and by Routledge
2 Park Square, Milton Park, Abingdon, Oxon, OX14 4RN

Routledge is an imprint of the Taylor & Francis Group, an informa business

© 2021 Taylor & Francis

The right of Kevin Phillips to be identified as author of this work has been asserted by him in accordance with sections 77 and 78 of the Copyright, Designs and Patents Act 1988.

All rights reserved. No part of this book may be reprinted or reproduced or utilised in any form or by any electronic, mechanical, or other means, now known or hereafter invented, including photocopying and recording, or in any information storage or retrieval system, without permission in writing from the publishers.

Trademark notice: Product or corporate names may be trademarks or registered trademarks, and are used only for identification and explanation without intent to infringe.

ISBN: 978-0-367-47822-3 (hbk)
ISBN: 978-0-367-47727-1 (pbk)
ISBN: 978-1-003-03669-2 (ebk)

Typeset in Minion
by Deanta Global Publishing Services, Chennai, India

To my love, Loida

Contents

SECTION II   Digging Deeper

SECTION III   Inside Your Organization

SECTION IV   What's Next?

Preface

Blockbuster is dead.

Borders Bookstore is gone.

Toys 'R' Us is on life support.

And since starting to write this book, Payless Shoes has filed for bankruptcy.

None of these former powerhouses would have ever dreamed that they would be out of business. They were all positive they were safe from the changes that were going on in their respective industries and believed they could easily coast through whatever turbulence they were experiencing. They were industry leaders and were certain they could do whatever they wanted because they were immune to everything that was happening around them. And because of this, they are either out of business or on the brink of collapsing.

It doesn't matter what industry, market, or business you are in; the extraordinary changes that are taking place in the world today have the potential to transform you from industry front-runner to liquidation if you are not able to adapt and evolve. However, while increased risk is present, the opportunity to reach great heights and capitalize on all of the changes that are occurring is also within your grasp. The key is transforming your organization to meet the demands of tomorrow.

This is not necessarily an appealing perspective, but it is the very nature of what has consistently happened over the past 20 years and will be occurring at an even greater frequency over the next decade. The business environment is transforming at a faster rate than ever, making it clear that complacency is a formula for failure, and the time for change is now.

If you are interested in transforming your organization in order to build sustained success, *Change and Execute* is the book for you. The author provides astute direction on how to increase productivity and optimize workplace performance, ultimately enabling you to produce better bottom-line results.

Acknowledgments

I am beyond grateful for all of the support, encouragement, and inspiration I have received throughout the development of this book. Specifically, thank you to my family and friends. Your love, kindness, and support were instrumental in putting this book together.

I would especially like to thank my parents, Katy Chafin and Dave Phillips, for your unwavering support and encouragement. Thank you also for being my editors and sounding board. Your continued support in my writing means everything. Thank you, Elaine Kramer, for your guidance and direction. Your vast knowledge, diverse experiences, and unique insights never cease to provide clarity and expertise when it is needed the most.

Loida Deynes, thank you for being so supportive throughout this entire process. Your encouragement motivated me to continue putting forth my best effort, and I am so thankful for you. I am blessed to share my life with you.

Finally, Productivity Press, and more specifically, Michael Sinocchi, thank you for providing me the opportunity to work with you again. I am honored that you were willing to take this project on.

Acknowledgments

Author

Kevin E. Phillips is a 2017 Top 40 Under 40 Military Honoree, Director of Strategic Planning at Envolve Pharmacy Solutions, MBA graduate of the University of Michigan's Ross School of Business, United States Air Force Veteran, Center for Positive Organizations Fellow, and Project Management Professional. For the past 15 years, Kevin has worked in various business industries and organizations providing strategic insights, solutions, and direction and knows exactly what it takes to build high performing teams, implement change, and transform potential into productivity. In addition to *Change and Execute*, Kevin has written two other books: *Employee LEAPS* and *Managing Millennials*. Both books focus on optimizing workplace performance.

Introduction

The only constant in business (and life) is change. No industry, market, company, or person stays the same. Instead, ebbs and flows naturally occur, with this inevitably shaping the way the world works. Technology is improved, processes are optimized, and employees find better ways to do their job.

This is not appreciated by everyone, especially industry leaders and those who are experts in their field. When you are winning the game, no one wants the rules to be changed. Yet the business world continues to adapt and evolve, with many who were once leaders suddenly becoming no longer relevant. Deep down, everyone knows to be successful you must change. However, resistance is still often present due to many companies (and people) being comfort-centered instead of results focused.

We want to maintain the status quo rather than make difficult decisions that require more work, so we convince ourselves that everything is fine and there is no reason to change. Business will continue to boom, employees will naturally fall in line and start producing better results, and our work will propel us back on top. If we are honest with ourselves, we know none of this is true.

The truth is, if you are not improving, you are falling behind, and if you are not getting better, your competition is gaining an edge. This has been and always will be the case, and is especially true in business today. Competition is fiercer than ever, with transformational shifts taking place in every industry, market, and company. This requires companies to continually adapt and evolve. No longer can organizations (or individuals) be complacent if they want to get ahead. Instead, they must continually improve, and do it as quickly and efficiently as possible.

So whether you are a Fortune 500 corporation or a one-person shop, a leader of thousands or a manager of a select few, or a member of a top-secret military team or a teenager working at your very first job, you must do what is necessary to differentiate yourself from others and increase the value you deliver to the customer. If you do not, you are at risk of being replaced.

Change and Execute: How to Transform and Design Your Business for Sustained Success has been written to help you do just that. This book provides strategic insights, solutions, and direction that will empower you to transform your organization by providing definitive actions that will increase productivity and optimize workplace performance.

Change and Execute has four sections. Section I is an introduction to the changes that are going on in the world today and focuses on the new challenges that have materialized because of these changes. It highlights the benefits of adapting as well as the perils that come along with the resistance to evolve. Additionally, it unveils four overarching questions that are fundamental to the development of this book. These four core questions are what every company (and employee) should ask themselves:

- What do you do?
- What could make you obsolete or replaceable?
- What change can you make to eliminate this risk?
- What specific actions can you take to execute this change?

Though simplistic in nature, these questions challenge companies to be transformational while simultaneously enabling them to produce extraordinary value. This will ultimately deliver better bottom-line results.

Section II delves into the dynamic transformations that are occurring throughout every industry and organization in the world and focuses on areas that companies must address to be successful. This section of the book enables the reader to gain a profound understanding of how the landscape of the business world has changed and how you must adapt to meet the new demands of the market. Areas of importance include delivering maximum value to customers and the increased threats that are now present due to a global market. The section ends with a case study on how the Golden State Warriors revolutionized the NBA. The study effectively draws parallels between how this team changed the way basketball is played and how business in the 21st century has evolved.

Section III looks inside the organization, paying particular attention to leaders, employees, and organizational productivity. Knowing that the external environment isn't the only part of the business world that changes, it is important to address the way organizations are transforming internally as well. Section III accomplishes this by taking a deep dive into the way people and workplaces are evolving and highlights key characteristics leaders, employees, and organizations must have moving forward.

Section IV is a call to action. Identifying how the business world has changed is valuable, but it pales in comparison to actually committing to a new course of action. This section places the onus of making change on the reader, with specific actions companies (and people) must take to win in the next decade. The section ends by addressing 10 changes that will transform the business world over the next 10 years. These changes are focused on technology, processes, employees, customers, and the workplace and are designed to help organizations take action.

Finally, there is an appendix that lists all of the companies and industries referenced in the book that have gone out of business, filed for bankruptcy, or experienced considerable loss because of their inability to change to meet the new demands of the market. This appendix displays the extraordinary importance of changing and executing.

Through it all, *Change and Execute* addresses challenges companies face while empowering you to strengthen your place in the market and transform potential into productivity. The secret to improving your business so you are able to deliver sustained success is in your hands. With that in mind, you are encouraged to use this book to transform your organization and take it to the next level!

Section I

Change and Execute

If you do not change, you will die.

The world and the people in it will always be in a constant state of flux, so the idea that a company is able to remain stagnant and be successful is false. This has been and always will be the truth, and requires you to constantly adapt and evolve.

This is even more important in today's world. Unlike generations past where change moved at a glacial pace, change now happens at lightning speed. Industries and markets are changing faster than ever before, making it necessary that you continually improve. This is evident from the many companies that have failed, including the likes of Toys 'R' Us, Blockbuster, and Borders Bookstore, to name a few. Their inability to meet the changing dynamics of the market resulted in their demise.

Many businesses can withstand adapting for the short term, but continual resistance will cause them to not only miss out on opportunities for growth, but quite often, eliminate the prospect of them remaining in business at all. This is especially true in today's climate. With increased use of technology, specialization at every part of the value chain, and paradigm shifts occurring faster than ever, change is not an option, it is a necessity.

Equally important to change is execution. There are no shortages of unique ideas that will conceivably transform industries, exciting plans that are sure to revolutionize business models, and talented employees capable of setting the world on fire. But knowing you need to change and taking action are very different. True value is only generated when the change introduced is acted upon and execution takes center stage. Execution transforms an idea into a business, converts a concept into a product, and brings a service to market. Everything that produces value revolves around execution.

For example, ridesharing had been discussed extensively for many years, but the founders of Uber and Lyft were the ones who made it become a reality. Similarly, people have always wanted to rent out the extra bedroom in their home, but Craigslist brought it to fruition, and Airbnb took it to the next level. And though grocery stores have provided consumers with fresh food for decades, the ease at which Amazon, Walmart, and other large corporations simplify the process through home delivery makes shopping a breeze. These improvements create exceptional value for customers while simultaneously flipping industries upside down.

This makes it apparent that, in order to win in this new environment, you must not only figure out how to change, you must also be able to execute quickly and efficiently.

1

The World Has Changed

In January of 1994, during an episode of *The Today Show*, Katie Couric asked Bryant Gumbel the infamous question, "What is internet?" The hosts, adept at discussing topics ranging from current events and new movie releases to politics and environmental issues, were much like everyone else in the world who lacked common knowledge about this new technology and what it could do.

Today, the internet is a foundational component of every part of our lives and serves as a vital resource in our ever-changing world. However, while the internet, and technology in general, has enabled companies to adapt and evolve, it has caused considerable challenges throughout the years as well. Change is difficult. It is much easier to travel down the same path you always have, remain comfortable in your current environment, and coast along a smooth trajectory than it is to change. This causes many companies (and people) to resist the need to transform their operation and improve their business. This inevitably leads to failure.

The world will always change, so the idea that you can hold onto past ways of doing business and approaches toward success is false. If you want to succeed, you must change.

IF YOU DO NOT CHANGE, YOU WILL DIE

Change has always been and will always be a part of the business world. The need to continually adapt, evolve, and improve has always been important. No company or person has ever been able to rest on the laurels of their past to deliver success in the future without making changes.

However, in this day and age, it is different. In the past, change was slow and occurred over time. This provided companies the opportunity to analyze change, make deliberate plans, and then methodically implement meticulous processes that carefully orchestrated a new way of doing business. Companies were able to make incremental changes over time, allowing everyone in the organization to be prepared for what was to come.

This is no longer the case. Change now happens at a torrid pace, with every company in every industry always looking for new ways to cut corners, reduce their financial burden, and get a leg up on the competition. And rather than experiencing small changes that were rolled out over a period of time, in today's environment, seismic shifts happen at a moment's notice. New products and services with transformative functionality cause disruptive change that can wipe out businesses and flip industries upside down. This eliminates the opportunity to be passive and wait for the perfect time to pull the trigger. Instead, companies must execute their plan of attack quickly and efficiently.

Not surprisingly, many businesses (and people) do not appreciate this harsh reality. They favor a slow, disciplined approach toward change, prefer to maintain consistency with their operation, and want tradition over transformation. For this group, the end is no surprise. Their business invariably struggles to compete as they miss out on the tangible benefits that come from improving their operation.

This is evident from the long-suffering pain companies like Radio Shack, Sears, and Xerox have experienced and is analogous to what countless independent bookstores, small hardware businesses, and vintage furniture shops have gone through. Though the reason for each company's downfall could be endlessly debated, the overarching theme can be summed up in a single sentence. The failure to change destroyed the opportunity to remain competitive.

This makes it simple. If you want to win, you must change and execute.

A BLOCKBUSTER FAILURE

Many established companies in mature industries are working tirelessly to hold on to the good old days and celebrate the successes of yesteryear.

Both huge corporations and small "mom and pop" shops choose to reflect fondly on the way things once were and how their business has been successful in the past, while resisting the need to transform.

These organizations are trying to hold onto past glory, believing the future is bright by looking in the rearview mirror. This happens when nostalgia sets in. The false sense of security created by reflecting on past memories creates a trap that has companies (and leaders) trying to replicate previous victories by copying what used to work. When you do this, you are breathing irrational hope into your organization.

These types of organizations don't want to admit that the world has transformed and that they need to adapt and evolve. They attempt to keep the same business model or push products and services that are no longer valued by consumers. Or they make small changes and minor tweaks, while not looking deep enough at what really needs to change. They irrationally believe that if they make incremental modifications, they will be alright, just like they have always been. While in the end these organizations eventually acknowledge the need to make significant change, quite often, they don't accept the gravity of the situation until it is too late.

This was the case with Blockbuster Video at the start of the 21st century. As the powerhouse in the movie rental industry in the 1990s, Blockbuster was *the* place to check out videos. The opportunity to go into a Blockbuster store to look through hundreds of VHS tapes and DVDs throughout the facility brought so much joy and happiness to movie lovers. With hundreds of films in stock, patrons could walk up and down the aisles perusing various genres, themes, and categories. And with 9,000 stores strategically placed all over the world and 40% market share, nothing appeared to cause the company much concern.

They were seemingly too big and powerful to be touched. Because of this, the company barely flinched when in 1997, Netflix, a hip start-up with a new business model of online ordering and delivery by mail, came on the scene looking to break into the movie rental business. Blockbuster was the perennial leader in home movie rentals and could conceivably do no wrong. At its peak, the company was valued at over $8 Billion.[1]

To add to Blockbuster's inflated ego and further cement their place as the industry leader, Netflix leadership approached Blockbuster in 2000 offering to sell their company to the huge corporation for $50 million. Top brass at Blockbuster declined, citing that Netflix was a "very small niche business."[2]

Blockbuster believed the path to future success would be built upon what they were currently doing and there simply wasn't enough volume in what Netflix was going after. This caused Blockbuster to double down on their business model and reject home delivery through use of the internet. This proved to be a pivotal turning point in Blockbuster's business and the start of a decade of futility.

Blockbuster's flawed mentality caused them to post net losses of $1.6 billion and $978 million in 2002 and 2003, respectively.[3] At the same time, Netflix was growing. In 2002, the company doubled its revenue from the previous year, generating over $150 million, and by 2003, posted its first profitable year. The young company earned $6.5 million on revenues of $270 million.[4]

Amid continual struggles and a growing online market, Blockbuster reluctantly joined the online DVD rental business in 2004. Over the next 2 years, they were able to amass 2 million members. But by then, it was already too late. The value of the company had dropped to $500 million. During the same stretch, Netflix continued to bolster its position in the market, eclipsing over 6 million subscribers while being valued at $1.8 billion, dwarfing the company that was once the definitive goliath in the industry.[5]

The end of the story is quite anticlimactic. In 2010, Netflix earned $2.1 billion in sales, while Blockbuster continued to spiral out of control. In September of that year, facing revenue losses of $1.1 billion, Blockbuster filed for bankruptcy. At that time, the company was valued at $24 million, down from $8 billion. In less than a decade, the company lost everything.[6]

This tragic saga is something no one could have predicted at the turn of the century, yet happened because of Blockbuster's inability to change and inherent interest of relying on past success to deliver future results. The company kept an outdated business model, believed no one could touch them, and scoffed at anyone who didn't blindly accept that it would overcome the desperate situation it was in. Even in the months leading up to filing for Chapter 11, senior leadership insisted Blockbuster was in a better strategic position than almost anyone in the market, while denying any financial troubles.[7]

Instead of reflecting on the risks to the company, assessing how the world was changing, and identifying a clear path for the future, Blockbuster died a slow and painful death. A story far too common in today's environment.

FOUR CORE QUESTIONS

Blockbuster's unwillingness to accept the need to adapt and evolve destroyed any chance of them succeeding when the market changed. They simply couldn't compete in the new environment because they did not want to let go of what enabled them to be successful in the past.

The willingness to remain fluid in a fast-moving economy is essential. Knowing how to leverage your core competency and being willing to adapt to the changing dynamics in the business world improves your place in the market and ability to have sustained success in the future.

Unfortunately, there isn't a surefire path that will guarantee success. However, there are four core questions that will help you get started moving in the right direction. These four core questions are designed to provoke thoughtful reflection, while helping you connect what you read with how you can apply it to your business.

What Do You Do?

Defining what you do (and what your goal is) should be the driving force behind all of your decisions. Fundamental to the core, this is the first building block to help you succeed. However, don't look at the specific actions you take or functional approach you employ, but rather, the value you deliver to consumers. For example, Blockbuster placed emphasis on convenient, well-stocked stores that offered a huge variety of videos in every neighborhood, but their true value centered on providing entertainment to customers. Their misplaced focus caused them to miss out on what was actually important. Do not fall into this trap. Instead, focus on your core purpose.

What Could Make You Obsolete or Replaceable?

Companies don't typically fail because they are unable to continue producing quality products or maintain a consistent level of service. Companies fail because competitors find a way to create value for consumers that eliminates their competitive advantage. This makes these companies expendable. If you truly want to win, find a way to make your current products and services obsolete (before your competition does).

By having this mentality, you will be driven to always look for ways to improve.

What Change Can You Make to Eliminate This Risk?

Stop thinking linearly. The answer to your problem could be moving directly from Point A to Point B. However, this isn't always the case. The solution could be outside the box. Especially in competitive industries with established products and services, the answer is quite often not a direct line. For example, Blockbuster looked at its current competition and took the initiative to have more selection and more inviting stores. That didn't matter. The issue was never about creating a pleasant atmosphere or having a lot of content. Rather, Netflix made it so easy for people to rent DVDs (and stream movies) that customers had no choice but to make the switch. The motivation to change had nothing to do with where Blockbuster placed their emphasis. The reason consumers stopped using Blockbuster was because it had an archaic business model that lacked relevance. Blockbuster missed this; they failed to recognize the disruptive change that came along. Rather than looking at problems from the surface level, dig deep! Determine the change you can make that will increase the value you deliver.

What Specific Actions Can You Take to Execute This Change?

The final step is actually implementing the change. This is often the most difficult part of the process. So many times, companies (especially mature companies in competitive markets) put off making changes because of the inherent belief they cannot afford to slow down operations or take a break from being productive. They must continue pushing forward at all costs for fear that if they stop, they will fall further and further behind. Fight against this mentality. This approach will have you endlessly bailing water out of a sinking ship until it is too late. If you want to stop sinking, bailing water isn't the answer; you need to identify where the boat is leaking and plug the hole. Determine what specific actions you need to take to make the change you identified. Then execute that change as quickly and efficiently as possible.

It must be noted, even when Blockbuster did finally change, the company still didn't succeed. Disappointingly, there isn't an exact science for how to ensure the changes you make will generate a fruitful outcome that includes extraordinary revenue, booming profits, and an endless flow of customers. Nothing in business is a certainty. However, the willingness to remain fluid in a fast-moving economy is essential and creates the best opportunity to improve your place in the market and build a successful company in the future. And using these four core questions will help you get there.

BRINGING IT ALL TOGETHER

Industries and markets continually transform. This causes many lethargic companies that do not adapt and evolve to fail. They neglect to make planning for the future an integral part of the business because it doesn't hold the same significance day-to-day priorities carry. This causes them to be beaten by progressive organizations that launch forward-leaning strategies. The truth is, it doesn't matter what industry, market, or business you are in, the reluctance to adapt and evolve destroys the ability for you to compete. To be successful, you must continually transform while finding new ways to meet the demands of your customers. Anything short of accepting this as the truth increases your risk of falling behind your competitors and going out of business.

NOTES

1. Top Accounting Degrees. "Netflix vs. Blockbuster." *Topaccountingdegrees.org.* www.topaccountingdegrees.org/netflix-vs-blockbuster/ (accessed September 20, 2019).
2. Friedman, Wayne. "Could Blockbuster Video Have Been Netflix?" *MediaPost.com.* www.mediapost.com/publications/article/316647/could-blockbuster-video-have-been-netflix.html (accessed September 25, 2019).
3. Securities and Exchange Commission. "Blockbuster INC." *SEC.gov.* www.sec.gov/Archives/edgar/data/1085734/000119312505063510/d10k.htm (accessed October 10, 2019).
4. Statista. "Netflix's Annual Revenue from 2002 to 2019." *Statista.com.* www.statista.com/statistics/272545/annual-revenue-of-netflix/ (accessed March 7, 2020).
5. Macrotrends. "Netflix Net Worth 2006-2019." *Macrotrends.net.* www.macrotrends.net/stocks/charts/NFLX/netflix/net-worth (accessed March 8, 2020).

6. Dazeinfo. "Netflix Revenue by Quarter: FY Q1 2012-Q4 2019." *Dazeinfo.com.* https://dazeinfo.com/2019/01/07/netflix-quarterly-revenue-worldwide-graphfarm/ (accessed March 10, 2020).

7. Carr, Austin. "Blockbuster Bankruptcy: A Decade of Decline." *Fastcompany.com.* www.fastcompany.com/1690654/blockbuster-bankruptcy-decade-decline (accessed March 10, 2020).

2

You Need to Change

In 2017, the World Economic Forum stated that 65% of children entering primary school at that time would ultimately end up working in jobs that don't exist yet.[1] Two years later, Oxford Economics forecasted that robots were rapidly on their way to taking 20 million manufacturing positions away from employees. This makes it clear that if you are not making a concerted effort to continually adapt, evolve, and improve, you will lose. There is no disclaimer and no exception. If you do not place constant emphasis on elevating your operation, your business is in trouble.[2]

This truth is growing increasingly important because the cycle of change has become so pronounced that it is deafening. Changes in the world are now happening at a faster rate than ever, causing businesses that used to be industry leaders becoming obsolete seemingly overnight. Companies simply can't keep up with the way industries and markets are transforming, and this is just the beginning.

Moving forward, your business will continue to become faster, busier, more complex, more integrated, and more technologically focused than ever before. This creates an undeniable reality – you must change. But knowing you need to change is not enough. You must take decisive action. If you do not, you will not be in business for long.

DIFFUSION OF INNOVATIONS

The willingness to adapt and evolve has always had pushback. While some companies (and people) are able to jump right in on the latest and greatest innovations immediately, others are more resistant, choosing to delay adopting and fighting change for as long as possible.

The varying levels of interest in changing and innovating are what is known as the *Diffusion of Innovations Theory*. This theory helps to explain at what rate new ideas or technology are adopted. This theory is not new, but it has gained considerable recognition in recent years. This is for a variety of reasons, but can be primarily attributed to the way the internet, and technology as a whole, has transformed the way businesses operate. Companies leaning forward are able to leverage progressive strategies and pioneering practices that have enabled them to capitalize on the changes that are taking place. Conversely, organizations that have undermined the importance of adopting change and modifying their operation have struggled.

Delving deeper, companies typically fall into one of five distinct groups within the Diffusion of Innovations Theory. The five groups are:

Innovators

Innovators (2.5%) are those who develop the innovation or set the bar for what everyone else must strive to achieve. They place extraordinary time, energy, and creativity into developing new, innovative products and services. They are willing to take risks and are comfortable adopting new ideas. These companies are always interested in pushing forward and believe they have the solution to all of your problems (and solutions to problems you didn't even know existed). Innovators sometimes seem idealistic and aloof. However, they have the potential to set the tone for an entire industry, as long as their head isn't stuck in the clouds.

How Innovators View Change

Innovators love change. They are always leaning forward and looking to improve their operation. They are not comfortable settling for business as usual, rather want to find ways to increase efficiency, improve speed, and streamline service. They are true champions of change and are always advocating for ways to improve their business.

Examples: Google, Amazon, Apple

Early Adopters

Innovators are followed closely by Early Adopters (13.5%). This group is forward thinking, maintains high social status, and has the necessary financial resources to be the first to act. Early Adopters pride themselves on adopting a new product or service after an Innovator has created it and seek the limelight for the way they are taking the lead. Similar to Innovators, these companies are often overzealous in choosing to adopt. They are typically "all in" once the benefits of the change are apparent, especially when they can see a direct correlation between the new product or service and the advantage they will gain from it. They enjoy being trendsetters and appreciate the social capital (and market share) it generates.

How Early Adopters View Change

Early Adaptors recognize the opportunities that come with making change to their business and so are willing to implement as soon as they see how it will be valuable. They may not be the one to come up with the idea, but love incorporating it as soon as possible. They appreciate how change can make their business better.

Examples: Walmart, The Walt Disney Company, Patagonia

Early Majority

The Early Majority (34%) adopts innovation after most of the bugs have been ironed out and the value is easily seen. These companies help innovation push past the tipping point to become more mainstream. They are practical by nature and are comfortable with moderately progressive ideas that have shown they can be valuable. However, the Early Majority often have financial constraints making them reluctant to invest until the idea (or technology) has been properly vetted. After the innovation clearly displays that it will generate value, the Early Majority buys into the product or service wholeheartedly.

How the Early Majority Views Change

The Early Majority aren't always seen as pioneers but do have considerable power within their industry. They make changes after understanding the value the change can generate. They are typically in mature industries and markets and cannot afford to fall behind their competition.

Examples: Large automobile manufacturers (e.g. Ford, General Motors, Chrysler), oil and gas companies (e.g. Exxon Mobil, Chevron, Valero Energy)

Late Majority

The Late Majority (34%) adopts an innovation after it has proven its worth. There is considerable skepticism with this group. Many in this group only adopt because they know they need to keep up with competitors. Being risk averse, the Late Majority is always observing their competition to make sure they are in line with those who are taking initiative and leaning forward. These companies follow mainstream standards and are constantly looking at what others are doing so they can jump on the bandwagon. Before buying in, they want to hear that the product or service they are adopting is a sure thing. Unfortunately, a big deterrent for this group is the negative influence they receive from the final group, the Laggards, who incessantly highlight what could go wrong with the idea or technology.

How the Late Majority Views Change

The Late Majority knows they will be in trouble if they do not implement change and so takes action to limit the risk of falling behind. Deep down they know they need to change but would love for things to remain the same. They are comfortable with the way their business runs, so they don't want to offset anything. This is often because they have had success in the past. Regardless, even the change they make may not be enough due to their inability to address all of the changes that are happening in their industry or market.

Examples: Sears, AOL, General Electric

Laggards

The Laggards (16%) pull up the rear and are the last to adopt an innovation or change. Unlike other groups, Laggards have a strong aversion to change and look to avoid it at all costs. They love tradition and always see the negative that could happen with any innovation. This causes them to postpone making changes for as long as possible, and when they finally do, they are usually kicking and screaming the whole time.[3]

How the Laggards View Change

Laggards only change because they are forced to change. They would love for things to remain the same and for them to be able to maintain "business as usual." They appreciate the way life used to be and wish their business would be able to just continue as it always has. Laggards will do whatever is necessary to avoid making changes. This inevitably causes them to fail.

Examples: Independent book stores, vintage furniture shops, small hardware stores

Being part of the Late Majority or Laggard group has always hurt companies. However, the increased rate of technological advances that is occurring in the world today makes it even more troubling. Companies that attempt to delay updates and advances for extended periods of time run the risk of falling behind quicker than ever before. And with new innovations such as artificial intelligence, automation, mobile platforms, sensors, and data analytics revolutionizing the way the world operates and business ecosystems function, and the pace expected to continue accelerating, the cost of putting off change is too much to ignore. In order to win, you must take advantage of the progressive way innovation is moving and business is transforming. You cannot afford to wait.

FOUR TYPES OF COMPANIES THAT FIGHT CHANGE

For those companies that are on the tail end of the Diffusion of Innovations scale, you must recalibrate. It is impossible to believe the world hasn't changed and won't continue to change moving forward. The technological advances, innovation, and new way of living and working make it abundantly clear we have merely scratched the surface of this transformational journey. Regardless, companies from every industry and market all across the globe continue to remain stagnant in spite of the dynamic shifts that are occurring in industries and markets all around them.

Analyzing from an objective perspective, there are four types of companies that push against what the market is telling them and instinctively fight change. Though they have different rationales for their actions, they almost always have the same disappointing outcome. The four types of companies that fight against change are:

The Deniers: The Deniers fail to acknowledge anything has changed. While they feel the pain in their finances, they can't understand why business isn't performing the way it once had. This has them continuing on with their operation without adapting or evolving. They push the same products and services and leverage the same mediums to market their inventory. Most Deniers have been eaten up by their competition by now. However, there are still businesses with deep pockets that fail to acknowledge the need to transform.

The Patronizers: Similar to putting a bandage on a wound that is gushing blood, Patronizers are not interested in making changes; they only want to make it appear that they are putting forth efforts. Though Patronizers are willing to acknowledge that there is a problem, they take the most evasive action possible. They do their best to sidestep any real change to their operation. This eliminates the opportunity to improve. In spite of their lackluster attempts, they are confused when their situation doesn't get better.

The Oblivious: The Oblivious focus on everything except for the real problem. They place emphasis on areas that lack true significance, concentrate on issues unrelated to the area of concern, and invest in solutions that will not improve their situation. These companies are like people who can't understand why their kitchen sink won't work after they buy all of the fancy upgrades and custom furnishings, not realizing that the pipes below the sink aren't connected to the well. The problems these companies are addressing run much deeper than they can see, yet ignorance creates an impasse. They don't know what to do to improve the situation.

The Resisters: If you are at home and you see a small fire in the kitchen, what do you do? Do you let it grow until it becomes a serious threat to burn your house down or put it out immediately? The answer is obvious. You spring into action and do whatever is necessary to minimize the damage that the fire can cause. While this is the case at home, in the workplace, Resisters try to wait as long as possible to put out the fire. Rather than taking action, Resisters bury issues because addressing them will be too much work. A lot of times, they will only acknowledge the need for change after it is too late, the industry has passed them by, and the market fails to recognize them as a true player anymore.

In the end, it doesn't matter which of the four companies you are when you are fighting change, the end result is almost always the same. You will gradually become irrelevant and die a slow, painful death.

Change isn't always appreciated. However, the benefits that come with adapting and evolving are the cornerstone for future success.

PEOPLE WHO DON'T GET IT DON'T GET THAT THEY DON'T GET IT

There are some people who just don't get "it." And worse yet, they don't get that they don't get "it." Such was the case with a delightful grandmother who heard the most fascinating news about her grandson, Mark. Mark, not yet 30 years old, was working at NASA and was assigned to be part of a project that was set to launch a satellite to orbit the earth. Mark put in long, hard hours and did whatever he could to make sure his piece of the project was ready for launch, and he loved every minute of it.

Mark's grandmother couldn't have been more proud. Her eyes would light up every time he would mention the work he was doing on "his satellite" and she told everyone what she could about her wonderful young grandson.

To be fair, why wouldn't she? Mark was working on a piece of equipment that would soon be in space orbiting the earth. However, for as proud as she was, Mark's grandmother got one thing wrong. Because Mark consistently used the term, "his satellite," she came to believe that he was responsible for the entire operation and that he had hundreds of people working for him. Mark was a valuable piece of the puzzle, but he was not in charge of the entire project; he merely had one area of focus.

To his grandmother, it did not matter. She believed Mark was in charge. It was his satellite. He was responsible for everything. In the end, people just allowed her to believe what she wanted to believe, knowing that arguing would never amount to anything beneficial.

This happens in business all the time. Reality is clouded due to the unwillingness to accept things we do not want to hear or fail to admit is true. There are still many in the world who believe the internet is not able to become more involved in people's lives, that their industry is not at risk of being disrupted, and that eventually, clients who left for streamlined service and lower prices will come back.

This is false!

The extraordinary transformation of how businesses operate and where customers place value will not change back. Rather, increased reliance on technology and streamlined service will be the heartbeat of virtually every decision every organization in the world makes. You are not an exception to the rule. It is noble that you want to keep things the way they are and believe that life was better prior to technology taking over, but the market has spoken and loudly proclaimed that it will never be the same. Everything has transformed and will continue to change, and this requires you to adapt.

Digging deeper, companies have merely scratched the surface of what technology will be able to do to enhance their operation. And as technological advances continue to be more intertwined with every part of business, this trend will continue to expand. So, for people who don't get it, and people who don't get that they don't get it, this is a pivotal time to reflect.

Change is happening faster than it ever has in every capacity of life, with no element, experience, or activity being exempt from this truth. For example, drones deliver packages to customers without human intervention, cars have sensors that turn the windshield wipers on when rain is detected on the windshield, and sports teams have rigorous analytics that highlight strengths and weaknesses for every player in every situation imaginable. Even something as benign as sleep has been infiltrated by technology. Various "Sleep Apps" track the amount of time a person sleeps, how well they sleep, and their average quality of sleep. All of these innovations were seemingly incomprehensible 20 years ago, yet now are commonplace.

This makes it inconceivable to believe that this trend will suddenly stop, slow down, or plateau. Rather, technological innovations, and more generally change, will continue to be a pivotal part of every business and become more and more integrated over time. Further, at no time in the history of the world has change ever occurred so quickly, been more important, or affected more lives than right now. This has industry powerhouses going from leading the charge and being formidable players to fading into the background and becoming obsolete, all in the blink of an eye.

While in the past, companies could delay changes and withstand fluctuations due to the slow nature at which everything occurred, that is no longer the case. Industries now turn on a dime, making once-impressive businesses suddenly grasping at anything that will keep them afloat.

If you don't get it, or you don't get that you don't get it, find someone in your organization who does and have them explain it to you (as many times as it takes). People who don't understand that you must adapt to the changes in the world or face extinction are in serious trouble. If you do not recognize the need to embrace what is affecting every industry and market in the world, you will be put out of business very quickly.

BRINGING IT ALL TOGETHER

When looking at history, powerhouse companies that have fought changes in their industry have inevitably fallen victim to others who have chosen to transform. From Circuit City and Tower Records to Blackberry and TiVo, the notion that one can simply rest on the laurels of past success and continue to thrive is impractical. Businesses unwilling or unable to pivot quickly and efficiently are being bypassed by companies that are able to think outside the box and implement solutions that leverage technological advances and progressive business practices, and this is just the beginning. Moving forward, new products and services will continue to transform industries, causing considerable fluctuations throughout the world.

You cannot rest on the successes of your past or even reproduce what your competition has created and think you will be able to get ahead. Instead, you must find ways to constantly be on the cutting edge of innovation and be willing to adopt new business practices to maintain your competitive advantage. The changes we have seen so far have been big, but they pale in comparison to what will occur in the future. You must look beyond what you have done in the past and place emphasis on discovering what you need to do in the future. What has happened in the business world so far is just the beginning. This makes it clear that you must change.

NOTES

1. World Economic Forum. "Chapter 1: The Future of Jobs and Skills." *Reports.weforum.org.* http://reports.weforum.org/future-of-jobs-2016/chapter-1-the-future-of-jobs-and-skills/?doing_wp_cron=1570340515.2430469989776611328125#hide/fn-1 (accessed April 6, 2020).
2. Oxford Economics. "How Robots Change the World." *OxfordEconomics.com.* www.oxfordeconomics.com/recent-releases/how-robots-change-the-world (accessed April 6, 2020).
3. Robinson, Les. "A Summary of Diffusions of Innovation." *TWUT.nd.edu.* https://twut.nd.edu/PDF/Summary_Diffusion_Theory.pdf (accessed April 6, 2020).

3

For Those Who Want to Win

Michael Phelps is the greatest swimmer in the history of the world! He competed in the Olympics 5 times from 2000 to 2016 and won 28 Olympic medals, including 23 gold medals.

His exceptional talent, chiseled physique, and internal strength and durability enabled him to become the most decorated Olympic athlete ever. Yet for all of the physical tools Phelps possessed, the one thing that cannot be overlooked was his work ethic. Phelps spent countless days and nights in the pool, working on his stroke and pushing himself to become better. This was for many reasons but was in large part because he knew that he could not maintain the status quo and continue winning.

This is evident based on the unique way swimmers have improved over the past 2 decades. Specifically, in the Summer Olympics from 2004 to 2016, Phelps competed in the 200-meter individual medley. In this race, swimmers must cover the four swimming strokes in the following order: butterfly, backstroke, breaststroke, and freestyle.

In each Olympics, Phelps won gold in the event. As impressive as that was, Phelps' Olympic Record time in the 2004 Olympics wouldn't have even gotten him a medal in the 2008, 2012, or 2016 Games.[1] Further, the gap between the first and last place swimmers from 2008 to 2016 decreased in each Olympics. The only reason Phelps was able to continually rise above the competition to claim victory was that he was willing to push himself to improve.

The same concept is true in business. For those who want to win, you must push beyond what you have done in the past and find ways to improve. There is no disclaimer, no alternative, and no excuse. The entire world is transforming before our very eyes, and if you do not get on board, you will be left behind.

This can be difficult to accept for many reasons but is often connected to the challenges businesses encounter when attempting to make a change. Rather than putting forth efforts to improve, companies rationalize how it is acceptable to remain the same. You cannot have this mentality and expect to win.

The revolution of change is occurring in every industry and market in the world. This requires you to abandon your steadfast ways of doing business for more progressive approaches. Though this causes concern for many, the alternative is much worse. If you do not adjust the way you run your operation, you will not be in business for long.

FOR THOSE WHO STILL DO NOT BELIEVE

Businesses (and leaders) that still do not believe they need to change are woefully unaware of the catastrophic danger they are in. The failure to understand that every organization needs to continually adapt and evolve to deliver value in this new business environment lacks basic reasoning.

However, this shouldn't necessarily be a surprise. An organization's resistance to change is often grounded in an urge to lean on what has enabled them to be successful in the past, with the belief that it will propel them forward in the future. Though not uncommon, it is a dangerous trap. This reckless thinking creates a false sense of security that the business will continue to flourish regardless of what the market does. The company will succeed (just like it always has) because of its competitive advantage, strong customer base, and deep pockets.

In theory this ideology makes sense, but it lacks practicality. The changes in the way business is conducted in today's environment make the actions you've taken previously no longer viable. Customers are only loyal to companies until a better product or service comes along or the price tag makes it advantageous to switch. Though you may push against this, it will always be true. Delivering maximum value at the lowest cost always wins.

For companies with outdated business practices, customary approaches toward how they operate, and inferior products and services, this is difficult to accept. While it has always been important to have good products and reliable services at affordable prices, in the past, the market provided the opportunity for established businesses to slide by so long as their inventory met the general needs of consumers. This was because there was a lack of visibility into alternative products and comparable prices.

This is no longer the case.

Customers are now able to easily filter through all types of products and services to find exactly what they are looking for at the right price. This makes everything you have done in the past obsolete.

Further, technological advances and progressive business practices have flipped industries upside down, leveling the playing field. Online ordering, digital marketing, and data analytics are just a few of the innumerable changes that have taken place that push businesses out of their comfort zones while minimizing the advantages that perennial industry leaders held onto for many years. And with new products and services being introduced at a faster rate than ever, the notion that you are able to simply reproduce what you or your competition have always done and have sustained success is wildly inaccurate. Yet these warnings go unheeded as companies choose to fight against progress while falling further behind.

So, for those who still do not believe, you are in danger. The changes that are occurring in the business world today will not stop. This requires you to take decisive action immediately. If you do not believe change is occurring, you will not be around for long.

FOR THOSE WHO LOST A GRIP ON REALITY

When you are succeeding in life, a common tendency is to take things for granted. The urge to push hard is replaced with an appreciation for what you have accomplished. This is often why sports teams have such a difficult time winning back-to-back championships. There is still a draw to win, but once you get to the top of the mountain, the passion for reaching the summit again isn't quite as intense.

The same can be said for companies that have been successful for extended periods of time. The desire to build dynamic products or cutting-edge services may still be present, but the success you have obtained causes your passion to diminish and excitement to wane. While there is still a desire to achieve greatness, the lengths at which you are willing to go do not stretch as far as they once did. Rather, you hold tightly to the success you achieved previously.

Whether we want to admit it or not, comfort breeds complacency. As a front-runner in an industry or a major player with a unique value proposition, the inaccurate belief that you can rest on your achievements without changing and maintain the same level of success is flawed, yet it happens all the time.

This is in large part what took place with General Motors, Ford, and Chrysler, leading up to their extraordinary financial hardships in 2008. The "Big Three" US car companies were at risk of potential insolvency without government intervention. There were numerous dynamics that went into why each was in such a dire situation, but everything centered on complacency and unwillingness to adapt and evolve. The Big Three had been thriving for so long that they failed to maintain a grip on reality or accept that they weren't the powerhouses they had been previously.

This was most evident when they came to the nation's capital to ask for public funds. Rather than coming to Washington, D.C., to humbly request taxpayer money in a conservative and respectful manner, executives from each company spent exorbitant funds flying in corporate jets. Though wanting a bailout, they refused to change their way of life. They acted like big shots while requesting special treatment. This gross misuse of finances displayed a sincere lack of acceptance regarding the desperate circumstances they faced. They lost their grip on reality and didn't want to accept the dreadful situation they found themselves in.

Bringing this to the present day, the tide of business is shifting, and the products and services you created in the past will not be what is wanted in the future. This requires you to adapt and evolve. Good companies understand this concept. They embrace the need to continue building on their competitive advantage to further differentiate themselves from others in the market. It is this very act of not accepting interim success as the finish line but rather just a snapshot in time that enables them to continue having success.

This approach could be unsettling but has the potential to enable you to continue winning. The extraordinary transformations that are occurring will not stop. This requires you to stop denying reality. Embrace the need for change and transform your business model so you are able to remain competitive.

FOR THOSE WHO HAVE ANALYSIS PARALYSIS

Deep in the woods many years ago, it has been alleged that a cat and a fox were having a conversation about how many ways they could escape their hunters. The fox bragged about having numerous ways to avoid capture, whereas the cat admitted to having only one. When the hunters finally arrived, the cat quickly climbed the tree to avoid the threat. The fox, on the other hand, analyzed all of his options but was unable to decide which one would be best. He was promptly caught.

This is synonymous with companies unable to determine a course of action because they have analysis paralysis or are half-pregnant with ideas but are afraid to move. Constantly overanalyzing and incessantly thinking about a decision but failing to create forward progress is the essence of futility. There are choices that should be made after careful deliberation, but, quite often, the time taken to assess the pros and cons isn't nearly as important as the time wasted on the decision. It is important to be calculated and maintain a meticulous approach when venturing into any new endeavor. However, when there is excessive discussion or unreasonable scrutiny causes delays, value is lost.

Quite often, being done is better than being perfect. Your ideas will always have imperfections, your plan will always need to be modified, and your team's processes will always require adaptations. The only way to discover what actions to take to fix these challenges will be to step away from the safety net of not making a decision in the first place.

It is certainly critical to analyze important decisions, but unnecessary deliberation will typically deliver uninspiring results or cause you to miss out on opportunities because you are too late. This is even more relevant today because of the disproportionate amount of information that is available. The amount of data that is now at our fingertips quite often drowns out relevant information.

If you want to win, stop being paralyzed by the inability to make a decision. It is important to discuss intricate strategies, implement efficient processes, and fine-tune how you will beat the competition, but overthinking a situation feeds into the law of diminishing returns. Conversely, taking a definitive course of action will generate quality bottom-line results. Instead of bouncing from idea to idea, assess your situation, prioritize your actions, and execute. It is the only way to succeed.

FOR THOSE WHO WEREN'T GIVEN A CHOICE

Sometimes, things come out of the blue that you couldn't possibly imagine; you are caught off guard by a competitor's new product, your facility is destroyed by a natural disaster, you need to fall in line with new government regulations, or you must find a way to recover from the untimely death of a key leader. Are you able to react to these unforeseen circumstances and recover? Or is this the end of the road for you?

Every company in the world had to ask themselves these questions in 2020 due to COVID-19. Originating out of China, COVID-19 is a strain of virus that had not been previously identified in humans. The virus is primarily transmitted by breathing in the virus when you are in close proximity to someone who is already infected or by touching a contaminated surface and then touching your eyes, nose, or mouth.

The ease of transference and relatively high mortality rate caused virtually every country in the world to have confirmed cases of COVID-19. Because of this, governments around the globe created strict policies that citizens were required to follow. This predominantly centered on stay-at-home orders and social distancing directives.

The pandemic caused every business in the world to adjust how it functioned. For example, restaurants could only serve takeout; grocery stores had strict rules for customers; and movie theaters, amusement parks, and entertainment centers were closed temporarily. Further, any business or role that was not deemed essential had to either change or stop functioning completely. Remote work skyrocketed, conference calls and virtual meetings became commonplace, and almost everyone who had to physically go into their workplace was responsible for wearing personal protective equipment.

In this unprecedented time, no one knew what was going to happen and no one felt comfortable. Even those who believed they had scripted out every conceivable scenario were caught off guard and lacked awareness of what would happen next. This caused thousands of companies to fold, millions of people to lose their jobs, and organizations throughout the world to transform the way they functioned.

How would pharmacies dispense medications? Airline companies transport passengers? And high schools and colleges teach classes? Everything was different, seemingly overnight.

Though another devastating scenario like this is not likely to occur again in the foreseeable future, this type of situation does happen to companies on a smaller scale all the time. A specific activity, scenario, or issue materializes that requires an immediate shift. The companies that are able to overcome the sudden transformations quickly and efficiently pivot their business and identify alternative ways to provide value. They thrive in the face of adversity.

For example, during the COVID-19 pandemic, large car companies began making ventilators, distilleries made hand sanitizer, restaurants converted exclusively to to-go orders, and yoga studios and fitness centers began hosting classes online. Disney World even streamed their fireworks to provide a glimmer of hope and cheer in this time of grimness.

Yet, for others, the catastrophic effects of COVID-19 proved too much. Neiman Marcus, an American chain of luxury department stores, had been in business for over 100 years, yet the challenges of COVID-19 overwhelmed the long-standing corporation, causing it to go bankrupt. In a little over 2 months, the once-highly esteemed company was waving the white flag so that they could restructure financially.

JCPenney, Stage Stores (that operates hundreds of Bealls, Goody's, Palais Royal, Peebles, Stage, and Gordmans), and J.Crew all suffered a similar fate. These companies filed for bankruptcy, closed hundreds of stores, and let go of thousands of employees.

At some point, something beyond your control will affect your business. For many, this sudden change has the potential to destroy you. If this is the case for you, you must take a step back and assess how you will absorb unexpected shifts and abrupt disruptions.

A sudden change in the workplace can be a captivating narrative. However, how you handle the situation is significantly more important. When you are dealing with a challenge that you did not see coming, appreciate the importance of transitioning quickly and efficiently. It has the potential to save your operation.

FOR THOSE WHO ARE STILL FIGHTING CHANGE

An ancient Chinese proverb states that the best time to plant a tree was 20 years ago. The second-best time is now. It is not hard to build a connection between this Chinese proverb and how it relates to your business today. The extraordinary changes the business world has gone through over the past 2 decades have placed an astonishing amount of pressure on every company in every industry and market. It has also challenged organizations to put considerable emphasis on meeting the demands of the new business environment so that they are able to succeed in their industry for years to come (so long as they continue evolving to meet customer demand).

For those who did not change to keep up with the market and instead are wallowing in frustrations and have a desire for things to be back to the way they once were, you must accept that this fantasy will never come true. Continually fighting against advances in business (and technology) only exacerbates the problem. You are not a victim of the changes in the business world, only a victim to your own unwillingness to be fluid and adapt to your surroundings. And if you choose to continue resisting, you are choosing to remain the victim.

Disappointingly, there is no easy button here. The world, and all that is in it, has created a cosmic shift that requires you to take decisive action. The world has changed, and with it, you must change as well. If you do not, your relevance within your industry and market will continue to fade away.

You need to stop justifying your actions and validating your every move. Refusal to make changes isn't a sign of commitment and strength to the old way of doing business but rather an example of stubbornness and obscurity.

To build sustained success, take ownership and execute the changes necessary to make your organization viable. If you do not, you will continue to fade into irrelevance while companies that invest in the future steal market share. Change is inevitable; your willingness to adapt to it is not.

FOR THOSE WHO FAIL TO ACT

If you ask people what the most important thing in their life is, you will inevitably receive a variety of answers. However, overwhelmingly, responses center on family, health, and religion.

All of these answers are noble, but they are missing something. You must actively commit to those parts of your life for them to be truly important.

For example, you could say you love your family, but if you do not put forth time and effort displaying that love and showing that you care, does it really matter what you say? Similarly, there are literally millions of people who express the desire to live healthy lifestyles, but the challenge of eating healthy and exercising prove too tall of a task for most. And while people claim to be Christian, Buddhist, Jewish, Muslim, or Islamic, quite often, many fail to live out their faith, choosing instead an easier path. At the very core, these activities have genuine importance, but without acting on them, they serve no purpose.

This is similar to business. Execution is the single most important element in every business. Without execution, you will never achieve sustained success. Conversation about a killer strategy is great, but without modifying your business model, you are stuck in the same spot. Brainstorming about a stronger online presence can be captivating, but not moving on an idea generates no value. And debating the pros and cons of a new marketing campaign can be interesting, but failure to pursue something different leaves you in no better position prior to the discussion.

This is exactly where many companies fail. It wasn't that Blockbuster didn't know customers were interested in receiving products via mail or over the internet, that Toys 'R' Us failed to recognize Amazon was stealing market share through online sales, or that Borders Bookstore didn't understand digital books were becoming increasingly popular. But it was these companies' failure to act that caused each of them to fold.

There is no benefit in endlessly mulling over potential changes you could make and no honor in looking back at all of the missed opportunities you let pass by. Ideas are the most common thing in business, so the notion that merely expressing a thought about a new business model, product, service, or strategy is equal to executing a change is woefully inaccurate. Instead, when no action is taken, reflection on what could have been is often met with regret.

An insincere approach toward implementing change in your organization will not garner the results you are looking to achieve long term if you do not put in the effort. So, while it is much easier to deliver motivational speeches, engage in corporate financial gymnastics, and maintain long-standing traditions that have bred company success in years past than to make difficult changes to the core of your business, it will not yield the positive results you are interested in. Superfluous actions and half-hearted attempts will not deliver success. In order to win, you must take action, you must execute.

BRINGING IT ALL TOGETHER

For those who want to win, you must change and execute.

The speed at which the world is changing and technology is advancing is beyond anything that has ever taken place. This makes it apparent you must always be ready to incorporate new business practices, technology, and innovation into your workplace. Reluctance to change, aversion to making tough decisions, and an unwillingness to execute will put your business in jeopardy. The opportunity to delay is gone. For those who want to win, you must take action.

NOTE

1. Youtube. "Bovell 200 Athens IM 2004." *Youtube.com*. www.youtube.com/watch?v=C9t5keinHik (accessed May 21, 2020).

Section II

Digging Deeper

In today's business environment, every industry and market has become more competitive than ever before. Every datapoint is analyzed, decision scrutinized, and product and service evaluated from every angle possible.

This is very different from years past. Businesses could often succeed on brand recognition or simply by being in the right place at the right time. Though it was important to produce valuable products and quality service, the inability for customers to see across industries and markets allowed companies with inferior goods to succeed in spite of their shortcomings.

This is no longer the case. In the ultracompetitive world in which every company is trying to squeeze out every penny in the value chain, organizations cannot hope to succeed unless they are constantly adapting, evolving, and improving. Customers now have more access to information than ever before and can easily gain knowledge about you and every one of your competitors. This enables them to continually find the best deal on the market. Furthermore, with specialization becoming so prevalent in the world today, anything you are not doing exceptionally well will be exploited by your rivals. This makes it necessary that you maximize the value you deliver to consumers at any cost.

This dynamic transformation will not lessen. Instead, you must accept that the landscape of business has forever shifted and the ability to maintain the same type of operation as in years past will not lead to the same profitable results. You must embrace delivering the most V-A-L-U-E possible to consumers, accept the new threats that have emerged because of the global economy, and determine the most practical approach toward executing change.

There is no debate; everything in business is changing. This makes it necessary for you to dig deep to identify how you can transform to meet the new demands of the market. To do this, you must place emphasis on the four core questions while reading this section:

- What do you do?
- What could make you obsolete or replaceable?
- What change can you make to eliminate this risk?
- What specific actions can you take to execute this change?

These are not the only questions to reflect on when reading this section, but they do capture the essence of what is important when building your company's future. To truly transform your business and create sustained success, you must discover the critical changes you must make to offset the new challenges that have emerged.

The global assault on every industry, market, company, and value chain is just beginning. Margins will continue to shrink, competition become more intense, and changes materialize faster than ever. This makes it evident that, if you want to succeed, you must not only adapt to the changes that are occurring today but also take a new perspective on what it will take to win in the future.

4

V-A-L-U-E

In 1993, *Jurassic Park*, a movie about a wildlife theme park filled with dinosaurs, was released in theaters. This was the first of many films in this franchise that involved intense scenes, hair-raising adventures, and exciting action that jumped off the screen. These movies had everyone sitting on the edge of their seat as they wait for the next encounter between the dinosaurs and the people. However, for as much success as the franchise has had, there has been considerable pushback; mixed reviews about plot development, debates over the actors cast in the movies, and conversations on whether the series has run its course are all endless topics of discussion.

Yet for all the negativity, to say that the movie franchise is a success would be a colossal understatement. The five movies released have already grossed over $5 billion worldwide, with the last two bringing in a combined $3 billion.[1]

Nevertheless, many moviegoers still express opposition to these films, stating they would much prefer something less mainstream. Viewers share they like going to independent films and watching movies with a storyline that is unique over a narrative with "plots they've already seen." These ideals are nice, but in the end, they are just banter. Millions of people flock to these movies every time they are in theaters to see what will happen next. Yet for as much money as the movie series has generated, the plot hasn't really altered for any of the five films. Broken down in the simplest of terms, each movie is about dinosaurs coming back to life and eating people.

The storyline isn't sophisticated, and it is no longer unique, but it does continually provide extraordinary financial returns for Universal Studios and is a perfect example of why the company is so wildly successful.

Universal Studios doesn't get cute or tricky; they just find products and services that will make them money and they push them to consumers. And with revenues averaging over $1 billion per movie, the company is not liable to stop developing new wrinkles in the Jurassic Park storyline anytime soon. Instead, rather than trying to pivot away from their competitive advantage, they add to it. For example, the marketing for the movie has been expanded, the special effects have been enhanced, and the mediums used to show the film have been upgraded. Virtually everything related to the final product has been improved to deliver a better experience for the consumer.

Smart, successful businesses identify valuable products and services, prioritize them, and get them out the door as quickly and efficiently as possible. They do everything in their power to simplify the process and maximize their return on investment (ROI). Though style, sizzle, and aesthetics are important, they pale in comparison to delivering substance. Great companies always maintain this understanding.

Alternatively, companies that fail to reach their full potential focus on products and services that are not in high demand, fail to place attention on value-add activities, and continually waste time and energy on areas that do not serve them well financially. They emphasize being right over getting it right and maintain a bias with their decision-making.

When analyzing from this perspective, it is easy to see how vastly different these two types of companies are and why certain businesses rise to the top, while others wallow in obscurity, or worse yet, fail completely. The truth is, in order to be successful, you must place all your emphasis on one simple activity, providing your customers with the most V-A-L-U-E at the lowest cost. Beyond this, nothing else matters.

But there in and of itself defines the actual problem. Glamour, appeal, and alluring ways to potentially generate funds overtake tried and true execution. Companies (and leaders) want to deliver the revolutionary product or service that will transform the industry yet fail to invest in prime areas that can generate quality returns.

This is not new, unique, or cutting edge, but the failure to focus on this simple concept destroys the ability for good organizations to be successful. Because whether we want to believe it or not, loyalty in business only exists when you can deliver more value at a better price to your customer than your competition. Once you are surpassed, the allegiance you think you have is gone.

SELF-AWARENESS, AUTHENTICITY, AND REALITY

Building a successful company is predicated on a variety of elements, with the recipe for success continually changing. In every industry, there are numerous components and unique workings that must come together to achieve a positive outcome and deliver maximum value to customers. While each industry is different and the tides of markets are always changing, there are certain elements that must always be present to win.

These fundamental elements allow companies to maintain a grounded approach toward leveraging their core competence, while simultaneously putting priority on dynamic activities that will set their operation apart. This ultimately delivers bottom-line results.

Unfortunately, this often gets lost because of competing agendas and alternative areas of focus. Though it is critical to maintain a zest for being cutting edge, and it can be important to continue developing new products and services that have the potential to generate revenue, the importance of balancing priority between who you are and how you will develop moving forward cannot be overstated. You must balance leveraging the competitive advantage you have with the disruptive changes that are taking place in your industry and market.

To maintain this balance, the three elements every company must have are: self-awareness, authenticity, and reality.

> *Self-awareness* is knowing who you are, what sets your business apart from the competition, where you are vulnerable, and the best way to maximize profits. It enables companies (and people) to have a balanced perspective of what the organization can expect to achieve without losing focus on what is important. By maintaining self-awareness, companies are able to place prominence on products and services that create value and avoid business ideas that lack practicality or fail to fall in line with what sets them apart. This enables companies to be mindful of boundaries while simultaneously enabling them to develop.
>
> *Authenticity* shapes the way companies manage their business. The willingness to accept that industries are changing and products and services are evolving provide authentic companies the opportunity to align themselves with the changes that are taking place around them.

They understand the importance of accepting the ebbs and flows of their industry and the need to remain fluid and agile. Conversely, companies that lack authenticity live in their own fantasy world and make the rules up as they go. Rather than admitting there is a need for change, they instinctively lie to themselves by using ill-advised data and faulty research that have been created to blur lines and sway opinions. Those that maintain authenticity understand that business is constantly changing and the ability to stay the same (and still win) is absurd. Those who fail to grasp this concept hold onto yesterday's glory, while believing it will bring tomorrow's success.

Reality comprises the willingness to accept that there is an inherent need to adapt, evolve, and improve. Companies that maintain a strong sense of reality embrace strengths, acknowledge weaknesses, and place emphasis on discovering how they can beat the competition while building on what has enabled them to succeed in the first place. It is reality that helps companies know in which direction to move.

By maintaining self-awareness, authenticity, and reality, you are able to remain in alignment with your core competency and set yourself up for future success. This eliminates the risk of straying away from your competitive advantage, placing importance on activities that lack true value, and accepting the belief that you can remain the same and flourish. You can instead focus on what is most important to consumers while remaining true to yourself. This ensures you will make appropriate changes at the proper time, enabling you to maintain your competitive edge.

Universal Studios figured this out with Jurassic Park; dinosaurs eating people causes millions of moviegoers to flock to the theaters. It puts butts in seats and makes the company an average of $1 billion in revenue each time a film hits the screen. By maintaining self-awareness, authenticity, and reality, Universal Studios is able to capitalize on the interest of their customer base while leveraging their talents. And though they venture off into new genres, explore innovative ways to meet the demands of customers, and improve their products and services through technological advances, in the end, they maintain focus on what is most important to their customer base and what will enable them to maximize their return on investment.

WE'RE NOT SELLING T-SHIRTS HERE, MOTHERF**KER

Yolanda was as colorful as she was charismatic, smart as she was unsophisticated, and passionate as she was persistent ... and she always had something to say. She would tell everyone about the guy she was dating, make fun of you because of the pants you wore, and let you know when you weren't pulling your weight on the job.

Yet, for as much of a character as she was, she knew what her role entailed and the value she delivered. Yolanda was the queen of getting people their medication. As a Patient Care Specialist for a small specialty pharmacy that shipped multiple sclerosis and cancer drugs to patients throughout the nation, Yolanda took great pride in making sure the patients she served got their prescriptions. She took the role so personal that when there was a problem, everyone who worked at the company knew exactly who to contact.

This was apparent one evening when Yolanda was working on a particularly difficult issue involving an insurance claim for a patient. She spent the better part of an hour working the issue to make sure the patient would be able to receive the prescription they so desperately needed. Unfortunately, just as she finished the claim and completed the order, Yolanda looked up to find that it was 5 minutes past cutoff time; the medication would have to be shipped the next day. Most reps would have waited, but Yolanda was undeterred. She submitted the order anyway and rushed down to the shipping department to ensure the courier would accept the package.

Unfortunately for her, the young deliveryman already finished loading his truck and made it clear that he had no intention of collecting any more orders that day. Yolanda didn't care. Before the courier could go anywhere, she told him that he needed to wait for the final shipment to be processed and loaded. To her dismay, he refused while expressing the importance of him staying on schedule and the company meeting the cutoff time.

This prompted one of the most heated exchanges anyone in the pharmacy had ever witnessed. The two went back and forth in an argument filled with anger and frustration seeping out of both combatants, with the exchange becoming more heated after each volatile remark. Finally, in a fit of rage, Yolanda screamed out, "WE'RE NOT SELLING T-SHIRTS HERE MOTHERF**KER! THIS IS LIFESAVING MEDICATION!!!"

At that very moment, everyone in the pharmacy froze as Yolanda and the courier stared deep into each other's soul. Finally, after what seemed like an eternity, the courier relented. He accepted the package and was soon on his way.

The truth is Yolanda understood the importance of her job and the value she delivered to patients. She knew exactly who she was, what she did, and why her role was so important. Yolanda was not just an employee who spoke to people on the phone; her identity was wrapped up in taking care of her patients, and no one did it better.

Many companies lack the perspective that Yolanda maintains. Rather than focusing on selling quality products, delivering exceptional service, or being a reliable brand consumers can depend on, they waste time and money on radical ideas that are outside of their capability, build business concepts that fail to fall in line with their core competence, and push products and services that are no longer in demand.

It is exciting to be involved in various endeavors. However, when the most important parts of business are pushed aside and the need to be productive is replaced with the desire to be sophisticated or stylish, you will lose. Knowing your value and understanding who you are and what you do is something companies all over the world fail to grasp, yet it is a cornerstone of having a successful operation.

In the ultracompetitive economy that we are now living in, there is a superior performer in every industry, market, environment, and location. To be successful, you need to know exactly who you are and understand the value you provide. This will enable you to place all of your energy on the problem you solve. You must be laser-focused on what your true identity is and how you deliver V-A-L-U-E to customers. Everything else is irrelevant.

THE ROI OF YOUR ACTIONS

There are times people place an enormous amount of emphasis on areas that aren't nearly as important as others, yet are more high profile, louder, or create a more significant buzz. For example, on average, there are six fatalities in the world each year from unprovoked shark attacks compared to one million people who die from mosquito bites.[2] Though there is an enormously higher probability of dying from mosquitos than from sharks, our focus is on the sensational over the practical; sharks are more captivating than bugs.[3]

The business world comes across this issue all the time. Companies place considerable emphasis on areas within operations that do not generate value while forgetting what has helped them become successful in the first place. We focus on the sophisticated technological advancement for a product that no one wants, innovative training platform that does not serve our employees properly, and ridiculous new service that affects less than 1% of the business. We laud over the employee who develops "brilliantly advanced" ideas that are beyond feasible and admonish those who come up with tangible concepts that are deemed not big enough. And we fail to place value on functional projects that could generate monetary gains for activities that are seen as pioneering yet lack practicality.

It is important to focus on the future and place emphasis on transforming operations to meet the demands of tomorrow. However, gratuitously concentrating on products and services that lack relevance, investing in areas that markets are not interested in, and developing cumbersome processes that fail to bring value to the company lacks common sense and is a superior waste of funds. Yet it happens all the time!

The harsh reality is no one cares about theory, philosophical discussions do not generate revenue, and moral victories are hollow. Practical application is all that matters. Functional execution is the only thing that is important. Business results that create value are the lone areas you must focus on.

Stop foolishly participating in activities that lack the prospect of having legitimate ROI. The ROI of your actions should be about delivering tangible value to your customers. Anything else is a waste of your time, talent, and resources.

MAKE IT EASY, NOT SEXY

We have all been in the presence of someone who has taken a picture of their meal and posted it on a popular social media platform with a funny phrase and catchy hashtag. Every one of us has met up with friends to grab a nice dinner at a fancy restaurant. And millions of people watch the Food

Network hoping to learn how to cook an extravagant dish. These activities are all flashy and what we like to highlight, but their importance pales in comparison to what is actually valuable.

Water is valuable!

Without water, you will dehydrate. Without water, you will hallucinate. Without water, you will die. Yet no one ever meets up with their friends to grab water, shares a picture of their water on social media, or watches the "Water Network" to check out new ways to drink water. Water is extremely valuable, but it isn't sexy.

In a world that glamorizes uniqueness and celebrates those who are able to transform basic activities into stimulating experiences, it is alluring to focus on new ways to spice up meals. Though being enticing in the restaurant business can be a great way to get people to eat at your establishment, this is not how businesses from almost every other industry should operate. Nevertheless, it is how many companies get into trouble. Instead of focusing on important activities that generate revenue, they place emphasis on flashy goods that do not have significant value or put energy into services that are not in high demand.

Typically, this materializes from an inaccurate belief that they must spend exorbitant amounts of capital to be successful. There is no question that money has the potential to open up doors for innovation, enable companies to invest in research and development, and empower leaders to create high-powered teams that have the capacity to deliver superior results. But it can also cause businesses to put money in areas that lack relevance and cause organizations to place significant effort on endeavors that are destined to fail. In these instances, money is not the gateway to success; instead, it is the jet fuel for the ego that causes poor decision-making and irrational behavior.

Uses of technological advances and creative innovation can be beneficial, but rather than just pouring finances into a product or service, objective analysis on the best course of action must take place. Though this is simplistic in nature, captivating (and expensive) ways to generate revenue or improve your financial situation can often overshadow alternatives that are easy and more beneficial, yet are not necessarily provocative.

There may never be a better example of this than one of the most successful (and simple) marketing campaigns that has ever taken place. In 2014, the "ALS Ice Bucket Challenge" was a movement that took over social media and touched every corner of the globe. Yet for all the commotion it caused, there wasn't a lot to it.

The premise of the challenge consisted of three actions:

1. Posting a video on Facebook of you dumping a bucket of ice water over your head.
2. Donating money to ALS.
3. Challenging friends to do the same.

This promotion was not elegant or fancy, yet was able to raise over $115 million in 2014, more than 15 times the amount of money that is typically generated annually by this nonprofit organization. The social pressure and peer recognition made this initiative a huge success. Individuals were going to great lengths to find the most unique way to participate in this bizarre challenge and were loving every minute of it.[4]

The Ice Bucket Challenge is an extreme example. However, it does highlight the importance of focusing on what moves the needle. It does not have to be sexy to be successful; sometimes even the simplest ideas can generate extraordinary results. So, while we all want to build extravagant products and services that will display our supreme talents, simple ways of delivering value can be a much better option. Because in the end, you must focus on the end customer and delivering value, not on how you or your company will personally shine.

MAXIMIZE THE VALUE TO THE CONSUMER AT THE LOWEST COST TO YOU

In the summer of 1988, a single mother of three young boys wrangled up her rambunctious children and piled them into the car to head out for the night. It was 6:00 pm on July 4 and she was determined to get a premier spot to watch the fireworks. The spirited family lived in a small town in a modest home and was surrounded by a tightknit group of neighbors.

Their house was about 4 miles from where the fireworks were to be set off, so it should have been an easy drive and fun night. To everyone's disappointment, it was not. It seemed everyone in the area decided to go to the park as well, causing massive traffic jams and frustrating delays.

The challenge for the woman was exacerbated by her three children, who clearly had too much sugar that day and were bouncing off the walls in the car.

To make matters worse, the day was hotter than usual, with temperatures peaking around 94 degrees. And though the family brought snacks to eat and water to drink, it wasn't enough. By 7:00 pm, two hours before the first firecracker was set to be lit, the kids were pining for more treats. This didn't bode well for the single mother who was on a tight budget and worked hard to keep food on the table and a roof over their heads. Nevertheless, she continually reached into her purse to pull out money to give to her boys so they could fetch more overpriced snacks from the vendor who was strategically placed in the middle of the park.

The fireworks were spectacular, but the evening turned out to be more trouble than it was worth. The terrible traffic, blistering heat, and expensive snacks turned what should have been a fun outing into an exhausting night.

The following day, the woman spoke to neighbors about her experience and was dumbfounded by what she heard. The neighbors stated they watched the same fireworks show, yet merely went out to the open field behind their house. They relaxed in the comfort of their own home, appreciated the wide-open spaces of the empty field, and enjoyed numerous refreshments they got from their kitchen. Frustrated and dejected, the woman thought about the amount of time and effort it took the previous evening, when she could have just as easily gone into the backyard to enjoy the Independence Day celebration.

This grim reality is too often what many companies experience. Rather than realizing what is important and doing what is necessary to meet the needs of the customer, businesses go above and beyond while creating no additional value. To succeed in this economy, you must only place emphasis on the specific actions that will deliver intrinsic and extrinsic value to your clients. More than just incorporating new technology, finding ways to be innovative, or developing a unique method of reaching your customers, the actions you take must be substantiated by the increased value you will deliver.

Stop wasting valuable time and resources on areas that your customers don't care about. It is important to leverage advances in technology and place emphasis on using innovative processes in your system but you must make sure it does not overtake the significance of delivering the most value to your customer at the lowest price possible.

Similar to the woman who spent more time, effort, and money to celebrate Independence Day without increasing the value of her family's experience, so too is it only important to place emphasis on activities that will be valued by your consumers. Anything that extends beyond this is a waste.

BRINGING IT ALL TOGETHER

The value companies deliver to customers has always been and will always be a moving target. Yet in the end, it is the only thing that matters. You must endlessly focus on being customer centric and discovering how your company's core competency can provide the most value possible to your customer. However, you are no longer able to stop there.

The pace of change in the business world today makes this the new baseline. To build sustained success, it is critical that you relentlessly pursue increasing the value you generate by addressing other problem areas as you continue to adapt, evolve, and improve. Your competition will never stop trying to upend your success. To combat this, you must constantly work to find new ways to increase the value you deliver.

This requires you to remain focused on looking at what the true pain points are for your customers, while knowing it will change over time. Be vigilant on where you place prominence and how change is affecting your industry and market. And more than anything, constantly work to identify new ways to create additional V-A-L-U-E for your customers.

NOTES

1. The Numbers. "Box Office History for Jurassic Park Movies." *TheNumbers.com*. www.the-numbers.com/movies/franchise/Jurassic-Park#tab=summary (accessed April 4, 2020).
2. Madden, Duncan. "The Annual Worldwide Shark Attack Summary Is Out." Forbes. com. \ https://www.forbes.com/sites/duncanmadden/2018/04/06/the-annual-world wide-shark-attack-summary-is-out/#1e717e981e9d (accessed April 5, 2020).
3. Hardy Diagnostics. "Who Is the Biggest Killer on the Planet?" *HardyDiagnostics. com*. www.hardydiagnostics.com/wp-content/uploads/2016/05/The-Most-Dead ly-Animals.pdf (accessed April 5, 2020).
4. ALS Association. "Every Drop Adds Up." *ALSA.org*. http://www.alsa.org/fight-als/ ice-bucket-challenge.html (accessed April 4, 2020).

5

A Global Perspective

From 2001–2010, the television show "Scrubs" was on the air as a medical comedy-drama series that followed the lives of employees at the fictional Sacred Heart Hospital. Each episode chronicled the good, bad, funny, and ugly that happens in a hospital, with unique anecdotal daydreams and reflections by the feature character, Dr. John "J.D." Dorian.

While Scrubs was similar to traditional sitcoms in many ways, it didn't always cater to television viewers with a Hollywood ending. Patients consistently died, relationships ended with heartbreak, and a feeling of sadness was often present at the end of episodes.

In an effort to add a new dimension and keep audiences intrigued, the writers of the show decided to include a unique twist in one episode by allowing J.D. to imagine what his life would be like if he was in a traditional sitcom. During the episode, a budget crisis required an employee to be fired, a patient was diagnosed with cancer and was informed he had only a short time to live, and a marriage was in peril. While this would typically be a dramatic and sad episode, that was not the case here; staying true to the way most sitcoms function, everything worked out. Somehow, the hospital miraculously found enough money to save the employee's job, the patient who thought he had cancer was misdiagnosed, and a single song saved the once troubled relationship.

However, just as J.D. was about to give his traditional end-of-show monologue to express how everything always works out, his daydream ends, and he is abruptly thrust back into real life. The next scene cuts to a beloved employee being fired due to a lack of funding, the patient with cancer dying in the hospital, and the marriage that had so much promise continuing to face obstacles.

This leads to J.D.'s internal dialogue about how things in the real world often fail to end as neat and tidy as they do in sitcoms. Rather, his time at the hospital is messy and difficult, and so too is real life.

Unfortunately, many people believe in the Hollywood ending that J.D. so desperately wanted in his daydream, especially when it comes to business. If their products could sell like they did when they first came out, if customers didn't demand the latest system upgrades, and if employees could work a little harder, then no tough decisions would need to be made and the company wouldn't need to change. This isn't reality nor is it how business works.

When you romanticize your company and attempt to hold onto past glory, you will not succeed. We are living in a more competitive, global environment than ever before. This requires businesses to change. Pushing products and services that are outdated, using archaic technologies that are no longer competitive, and fighting automation for manual labor are all signs of a company that will not compete long term because they fail to accept that the world has transformed.

If you choose to stay the same, you are choosing to not meet the demands of your current and future customers. This will ultimately lead to your demise. To build long-term success, you must fight against the urge to remain stagnant and align yourself with what it will take to win in the future. This requires that you ask yourself tough questions while maintaining an objective point of view when answering.

HOW HAS THE GLOBAL ECONOMY CHANGED YOUR INDUSTRY?

Products and services are easy to sell when you are the only game in town. However, when competition increases, the once easy business transactions are suddenly more difficult. Increased competition creates the need to make dynamic products and innovative services that stand out from the crowd. While you may be able to continue making money and capable of moving some of your inventory without changing, it will no longer be as quick and easy, nor as profitable. To win today, you must market more aggressively, showcase how you are different from your competition, and create unique ways to generate value for consumers.

Many businesses have learned this firsthand. They used to be the only hardware shop in town, retail store in the area, or electronics company with customer support in the region. They had the market cornered, and everyone had to go through them.

Life is different in this day and age. The idea that you will be able to easily hold onto customers and casually grow market share is woefully inaccurate. This is for many reasons, but quite often it is because of the extensive reach companies from all over the world now have. In the past, businesses were not able to easily acquire customers located out of their area. Though it was still possible to win business, it took a lot of time and effort to beat small, local companies.

In today's environment, businesses are able to encroach on your local customer base without being in your backyard. The internet has leveled the playing field. Proximity to customers is no longer the competitive advantage it once was. Every business now must compete on price and quality more than ever, making those that once had a competitive advantage due to their location suddenly needing to recalibrate.

This increased transparency has resulted in an extraordinary number of small businesses suddenly being on the outside looking in. In spite of this, many still fail to accept the need to change. They rely on atypical spending habits and unusual spikes in business to keep their company alive. The most glaring example is their reliance on "Small Business Saturday." Small Business Saturday is an American shopping holiday held on the Saturday after Thanksgiving in which people are encouraged to support small, local businesses. This is a great concept in theory but has become problematic in recent years.

Many small businesses have become so reliant on Small Business Saturday that it has become less of an opportunity for companies to showcase their amazing products and services and more of a day that organizations need to survive. The idea of using Small Business Saturday to generate revenue is great, but if you are relying on it to enable you to stay alive, your company is no longer relevant. You need a new strategy, business model, marketing plan, or product line to be viable.

Technology and transparency have created an opportunity for an influx of competitors to join the hunt and find ways to steal market share. Though not appealing, your once sought-after merchandise is now just a part of the mix due to numerous competitors that are all angling to get a piece of the pie. This makes it apparent that you must find a new way to differentiate yourself to be able to have sustained success.

WHAT IS YOUR COMPETITIVE ADVANTAGE TODAY?

When was the last time you went inside a gas station to pay for gas, checked to make sure the phone you were about to buy has a camera, or asked the concierge at the hotel if they had Wi-Fi? These amenities used to be highly coveted, dynamic variables that made businesses stand out. Today, gas stations everywhere have pay-at-the-pump, every new phone has a camera, and every hotel worth staying at has Wi-Fi.

Competitive advantages are in a constant state of flux. Rapid innovation makes once dynamic variables into market necessities. Many businesses don't understand this. They try to push outdated and overvalued amenities. They inaccurately believe their once coveted products and services will help them win market share. In reality, it just highlights the company's failure to understand the current landscape of their industry. They are attempting to live in the past and are afraid to make changes for the future.

Everything has a shelf life, with once dynamic variables transforming into standard features that provide no real competitive advantage. This challenges companies to continuously improve. Some businesses become frustrated by this notion. However, it does not change the reality of the situation nor does it allow you to remain static in an otherwise dynamic environment with realistic expectation that you will continue to win.

This can partly be attributed to the options that are now available in every industry and market. In the past, consumers would often accept products and services that were less than perfect because they had limited options. The internet makes this no longer the case. Customers now have more alternatives to choose from and are more educated about products and services. This enables them to be more selective with their decisions. This increase in buyer power reduces the willingness to settle for anything less than being perfectly satisfied and has caused massive disruptions in every industry and market.

Digging deeper, the competitive landscape has become even more convoluted due to nontraditional threats entering the fold. This is easily seen in the way Airbnb took on the hotel industry. Specifically, hotels had been the leader in temporary lodging for numerous decades while maintaining a fairly static business model. This was primarily because they never truly had a formidable opponent outside of other hotels.

However, as comfort and personalized service became more mainstream, guests at hotels suddenly refused to accept the way they were treated. Guests wanted a customized, hospitable experience. This was far beyond what hotels were prepared to deliver. Hotels were built around structure: breakfast ends at 10:00 am, the pool closes at midnight, extra towels are available at the front desk, a parking pass allows access to the garage, and a generic website with nondescript pictures and bland information all highlight order and a lack of differentiation.

This is very different with Airbnb. At Airbnb, you can eat whenever you would like, enjoy amenities without worrying when they will close, take advantage of the unique accommodations the property has to offer, and park in the driveway, just like at home. And rather than having to worry about the unknowns that a hotel could bring, Airbnb websites are all unique. Custom web pages, dynamic pictures, and distinct descriptions of every property are created by the host, offering a wide variety of options for consumers, and making it clear what you can expect. Airbnb hosts deliver personalized service and keep things as simple as possible. These attributes have become their competitive advantage, while enabling the company to attract a mass of customers and revolutionize an industry.

This is happening in every industry and market throughout the world. For example, large retail stores have always fought over market share with each other, so changes haven't caused many considerable shakeups. However, Amazon's entrance completely disrupted the industry due to their ability to cut cost and streamline service. Similarly, traditional gyms, fitness centers, and yoga studios had a somewhat isolated competitive landscape. However, innovative workout solutions like P90X and Daily Burn and cutting-edge fitness programs like CrossFit and Orangetheory provide new ways to get fit, while simultaneously disrupting the industry.

Static competitive advantages do not last. Attractive alternatives with legitimate differentiation can swoop in and steal market share. This can cause large companies to go from industry titans and market leaders to corporate laggards and irrelevant players in the blink of an eye. To remain viable, you must be agile and flexible with your approach and must always be looking to update and upgrade. Do not lean on variables that used to be important. Place emphasis on reinventing yourself and identifying how to continue to set yourself apart from the rest. It truly is the only way to remain on top.

WHAT ARE YOU WASTING MONEY ON?

Prior to retirement, John used to work a combined 80+ hours every week at his two jobs. During the day, he was a Sales Rep at an automobile supply company, selling engine parts to dealerships. After putting long hours in at the office, he would typically head home, eat dinner, spend time with his family, and then go to the firehouse at midnight. As a firefighter for the town, he worked the overnight shift from midnight to 8:00 am.

There is no denying that being a firefighter can be one of the most difficult and stressful jobs in the world. However, that was not the case for John. Though always willing to step up and head straight into danger, John's number was rarely called. The small, rural township he lived in and worked for had very few residents and almost no businesses. This had John spending most of his graveyard shifts sleeping at the firehouse. More often than not, during the nights John worked, he would kiss his wife goodnight, go to the fire station, and get a good night's rest. He was almost never called into action.

A few years after John retired, leaders of the township analyzed the Fire Department's operation and realized it could be more efficient by rearranging the way firefighters were scheduled. The township restructured policies and adopted what many other municipalities began doing, using 12- and 24-hour shifts. This saved the township money and improved the quality of life for firefighters.

Every organization has policies and procedures that lack common sense and are a waste of money. This is hard for many people to acknowledge. No one wants to admit they are misusing funds, failing to place priority in areas of importance, or focusing on issues that lack relevance. So, they mask their shortcomings. They tell you they feel more accomplished putting in the extra time and effort to manually load the machine, run the report, or build a prototype. They say adding a new piece of equipment that improves cycle time is unnecessary. And they validate overstaffing and hold onto longtime employees for sentimental reasons. All of these actions are nice in theory, but they are not justified if you are trying to win in the 21st century.

Failing to automate isn't a display of diligence and commitment, it is a sign of laziness. Not purchasing a new piece of equipment doesn't typically show prudence and responsibility, it highlights an unwillingness to invest in the future. And holding onto employees who are not producing value is not a sign of compassion, it is a display of weak character.

Competition has increased across every part of the value chain due to the global economy. This eliminates the opportunity to remain stagnant. In order to succeed, you must stop being complacent and start embracing ways to optimize your system, cut unnecessary waste, and improve your process. Whether that includes manufacturing, technical operations, or employee activities, the only way you will win is if you are willing to eliminate unnecessary spending in all its forms: time, resources, and people.

WHY ARE YOU TRYING TO OUTTHINK THE ROOM?

Every industry and market is now packed with numerous competitors, with the narrowest of margins often separating success from failure. This makes it critical that you stay focused on your brand and be committed to your expertise, while simultaneously listening to your customer base. This is not new or revolutionary but is consistently missed by companies.

This was evident with a plastic-injection molding company that made recycling bins for cities and towns. Started in the 1980s, this company joined the market at the perfect time. With recycling becoming increasingly important and communities taking a more active role in reducing excess garbage going to the dump, the business landed contract after contract with limited opposition and extraordinary margins. They rode this financially lucrative wave for over 2 decades. However, as the industry evolved and new competitors emerged, the fight to win business became more intense.

To set themselves apart, the company decided to install Radio Frequency Identification (RFID) Tags on every one of its recycling bins. This technology would enable communities to track the location of their bins, learn how much residents were recycling, and follow the route trucks took. This seemed to have considerable benefits, and at less than $3 per RFID Tag, could be installed at a fairly cheap price.

Adding RFID Tags to each recycling bin seemed to be a good idea, but after speaking with numerous clients and doing elaborate research, it was clear the customer didn't care about these benefits. The cost of the cart was the number one reason for purchase, not added technology or the ability to monitor how much recycling was being collected. The company ignored what the customers said and continued placing RFID Tags on bins. This caused them to miss out on numerous contracts due to the price.

Ten years later, the RFID Tags are still being placed on the recycling bins, and communities still don't care. Tracking recycling is not appealing or relevant, nor does it rank as a prominent driver for purchase. It is a waste of time and money.

In the cutthroat world that we live in and the global competition that we all face, the notion that you have the liberty to invest money into something that does not yield value to consumers is mistaken. Though some people will say it is important to push the envelope and show customers the value of innovative products and why they need to invest in cutting-edge services, more often than not, this line of thinking does not end well. If there isn't a driving force pushing you in a certain direction, you should not invest time and resources to head down that path.

Stop trying to outthink the room.

There will always be areas that you believe are important to focus on, but in the end, they do not matter if your customer disagrees. The most prominent driver for developing a new product, service, feature, or amenity should not be based on what you want. Instead, it must address what is important to consumers. This requires you to focus on your identity and listen to whoever is buying your products and services. If you are constantly trying to outthink the room, you will lose.

WHERE DO WE GO FROM HERE?

We've all seen it on the news, many of us have witnessed it exploring on vacation, and a few of us have even lived through it. It is the small town that was once a bustling metropolis. The decrepit area in the business district with dozens of abandoned buildings that used to be ranked as one of the best places to work. And the washed-out city that previously served as the home of a powerhouse in an industry.

What happened?

Why did everything fall apart?

What changed?

The truth is, everything changed, except for that small town, that area in the business district, and that washed-out city. And because of this, that location is suffering.

Industries and markets are constantly transforming, making it necessary that companies adapt, evolve, and improve. This concept is unsettling for many businesses, especially for those that are in front. When you are winning the game, the last thing you want is for the rules to change. It is much easier to ride the wave of success. This causes companies to go blind to the changes that are happening all around them. Truth is overshadowed by emotions, clouded judgment, and subjectivity. Rather than accepting facts and objectively analyzing your business, industry changes, and unique trends that materialize, leaders make decisions based on what they want to be true. This broken practice destroys the opportunity to deliver positive results.

To be successful, ill-advised decision-making based on subjectivity and personal interests cannot be a part of the equation. Instead, impartial analysis must take place, with specific focus on transforming to meet future customer demand. This comprises analyzing how the global market is evolving, avoiding the belief that the good old days are going to make a resurgence, and placing emphasis on setting aside egos in order to focus on what is most important moving forward.

Some companies have been able to keep their doors open while maintaining a stagnant business model in spite of the market navigating away from their core competence. However, the overwhelming majority has lost and will continue losing. Though you may have been able to acquire considerable market share years ago with a certain business model or product line, singing about past glory is not going to get you anywhere today. You must transform your products and services to meet the demands of the future.

The landscape of the business environment now encompasses global challengers at every level. You are no longer competing with traditional businesses in your local market, but rather, companies throughout the world. This global shift requires you to focus on what will sell in the future, while avoiding the temptation of doing what used to be valuable in the past. It truly is the only way to remain viable moving forward.

BRINGING IT ALL TOGETHER

The globalization of business has created new ecosystems in virtually every industry, market, location, and environment in the world. Because of this, the pillars from which companies built their success on are no longer relevant. You cannot function as you always have and continue to thrive. The competitive landscape has increased to a global scale. This requires you to recalibrate.

You need to stop celebrating past successes and naively believing that they will carry you to future glory. Eliminate investing in old business models that lack relevance in today's society and reject pushing products and services that are outdated and lack value in the market. Instead, you must transform.

Even if you have made significant changes in recent years, the notion that you are finished is wrong. The global economy we are now a part of is in constant motion and continually transforming. This requires you to maintain the same pace. The value you created for customers in the past served its purpose, but it is no longer enough. Decisive action focused on generating new value is necessary to thwart off global opposition and continue winning.

6

Change, Execute, and the Golden State Warriors

Romanticizing glory days, embracing business strategies that are outdated, and continually forgiving poor performance because of previous successes are the surest signs of a company destined to fail. Though this would seem obvious, remaining sentimental to what worked in the past and failing to adapt to the business environment of the future is an epidemic that pulses through every industry and market in the world. Go ask the former executives of Blockbuster, Toys "R" Us, or Borders Bookstore about not needing to adapt and maintaining the status quo.

There were many reasons these companies took a nosedive, but a lot of it revolved around the fact that they believed they were too big, too strong, and too untouchable to ever be affected by the changes that were taking place all around them.

They could not have been more wrong. No one is above the changing tides of business, and anyone who believes they are is in serious trouble. Companies must adapt, evolve, and improve to be successful. If they do not, they will die.

When thinking about this holistically, every company falls into one of two categories:

- Companies that recognize their business needs to transform to meet the demands of today (and tomorrow) to be successful.
- Companies that believe what they have done in the past and what they are doing now will work in the future. There is no need to change.

These philosophies are polar opposites, and though it is fairly obvious what type of company will be successful and which will falter, there are still those who lack the willingness to make changes, choosing instead to maintain the same course of action they have always had. These divergent approaches parallel many professional sports teams. Some teams are able to successfully use the unique talents of players and excellent leadership of coaches to capture multiple championships, while others consistently underperform.

A great example of this involves how the NBA's Golden State Warriors transformed the way they played basketball en route to winning multiple championships. This team's transformation aligns closely with how successful companies adapt, evolve, and improve to deliver results.

More specifically, the Golden State Warriors won the NBA Championship in 2015, 2017, and 2018. However, they didn't win by simply falling in line with the way other teams played. Instead, they identified unique ways to leverage the talents and abilities of their players and developed their own brand of basketball that took the league (and the world) by storm. This helped them become one of the most dominant teams in NBA history, while simultaneously revolutionizing the game.

It is clear there are vast differences between basketball and the changes that are occurring in the business world, yet the overarching concept is the same: an inflexible strategy and unwillingness to adapt will lead to a consistent inability to compete and the deterioration of your organization.

Conversely, objectively analyzing dynamic fluctuations in the market and transforming your operation to optimize performance will enable you to beat your competition. This can be seen in every part of the success the Golden State Warriors had and aligns with how companies that change are able to produce extraordinary results while businesses that maintain the status quo are destined for disappointing outcomes.

TRANSFORM YOUR GAME

Throughout the history of the NBA, it was always important to have quality big men that could be an intimidating presence on the floor. For as long as the NBA had been in existence, teams almost always needed a center or power forward down low to win. From the likes of Bill Russell, Wilt

Chamberlain, and Kareem Abdul-Jabbar in the 1960s, 1970s, and 1980s, to Hakeem Olajuwon, David Robinson, and Karl Malone in the 1990s and 2000s, there were few exceptions in which teams could excel without having a traditional center or power forward. Even as recently as 2010, the league was dominated by big, strong, muscular players like Shaquille O'Neal, Tim Duncan, and Lebron James. In fact, from 1991–2010, all but one team that won the NBA Championship in that span had a big man in the front court who would eventually make the Hall of Fame.

These extraordinary athletes outmatched their counterparts and imposed their will with the unique physical gifts they possessed. This style of game extended beyond just centers and power forwards. Point guards, such as Derrick Rose and Russell Westbrook, both drafted in 2008, relied on strength over finesse to dominate opponents. Flying through the air with reckless abandon, Rose and Westbrook attacked the basket every chance they got, and were respected among the league for being the fiercest of competitors.

This created quite a problem for the Golden State Warriors. The Warriors, a perennial loser that had only made the playoffs once from 1995 to 2009, didn't have these types of players. Though they had a few men on their roster with some talent, no one was a dominant force.

This made their draft of Stephen Curry, a thin-framed, 21-year-old with boyish good looks from little-known Davidson College, in the 2009 NBA Draft confusing. Curry had a smooth jump shot and amazing handles, but at 6' 3" and 180 pounds, he wasn't liable to strike fear into his opponents, let alone be a pivotal piece of the Golden State Warriors rebuilding process. To win, you needed strength and power; it was that simple. Regardless, the team selected Curry as the seventh pick in the NBA Draft.

Over the course of the next three years after the 2009 draft, the Golden State Warriors continued to languish in obscurity. They won less than half of their games each season, and no one was surprised. However, at the beginning of the 2012–2013 season, the team made significant improvements. They doubled their win total from the previous year and reached the playoffs for only the second time in 19 seasons. Further, with another flashy shooter in Klay Thompson (drafted in 2011), they were starting to make strides toward becoming a better club.

Nevertheless, after a lackluster performance in the playoffs after the 2013–2014 season that ended with a first-round loss to the Los Angeles Clippers, the Golden State Warriors fired Head Coach Mark Jackson and replaced him with Steve Kerr. Kerr, a five-time NBA champion as a player (three with the Chicago Bulls and two with the San Antonio Spurs), was a prominent guard in the 1990s and 2000s and holds the record as the most accurate 3-point shooter in NBA history.

The teams Kerr played for had progressive offensive strategies that involved motion, spacing, and tempo. Players were taught to read and react to defenses, with every pass and cut having a specific purpose. When executed properly, this resulted in open teammates, easy baskets, and ultimately, a more unified approach to winning.

His experiences on the court proved to be invaluable to the organization. Upon starting his role as the coach of the Warriors in the 2014–2015 season, Kerr noticed the extraordinarily talented bunch of long-range shooters he had on his squad and immediately placed a premium on offensive efficiency. He did this by taking the lessons he learned as a player and merging them with the deadly 3-point abilities his players possessed.

This strategy enabled the Warriors to win 21 of their first 23 games and compile a 67-15 regular season record, en route to their first NBA Championship in 40 years. The following year they won 73 games in the regular season (an NBA Record) before losing in the finals, then followed that up with back-to-back NBA Championships in 2017 and 2018. And they did all of this without a dominant presence in the low post.

The Golden State Warriors' use of the 3-point shot changed the game. Every other team saw how much success the Warriors had and knew they could not compete unless they changed the way they played as well. Shortly after the Warriors started having success, every team became fixated on the 3-point shot. To provide context, in the 2013–2014 season, the year before Steve Kerr became the coach of the Golden State Warriors, every team in the league attempted less than 27 3-pointers per game. In the 2019–2020 season, every team in the league shot more than 27 per game.[1]

Bringing this to business, many struggling companies inaccurately believe they are above all of the changes that are affecting every industry and market in the world and so avoid adapting and evolving. Rather than modifying their approach, companies quietly wait for the storm to pass and the fluctuations of the market to subside. They believe while there have been tough years that caused challenges they did not anticipate, it will not last; there is no need to change and the company will recover.

This is wrong. The transformations you are seeing in every industry and market make it clear that the world has changed, and the need to change with it is present. Companies everywhere are leveraging technology to take their business to the next level, and if you do not do the same, you will be left in the dust. So just as the 3-point shot transformed the way NBA teams now play basketball, so too has the internet, and technology in general, changed the way businesses operate. And with transformations expected to continue occurring in every industry and market throughout the world, the necessity of rising to the occasion to meet or beat the change head on is real.

STOP DENYING THE TRUTH

In today's NBA, firepower from beyond the 3-point line has become pivotal to success. This wasn't always the case; however, as the skill level of players has improved, it was clear the game needed to change. The Warriors, and more generally, the entire league has become so proficient with the 3-point shot, it was foolish to maintain the same approach that was used in the past. Even legendary shooters that had historically amazing careers couldn't match up to the talents players in today's league possess.

To provide context, the legendary Larry Bird played in the NBA from 1979 to 1992. Bird was known for being an incredible 3-point shooter. Competitors would cringe at the sight of him pulling up from behind the 3-point line, knowing that it would inevitably find the bottom of the net. Some experts still argue that he is the best 3-point shooter of all time.

Yet for as talented as Bird was, looking exclusively at the numbers, he is only the 147th most accurate 3-point shooter in league history (as of the start of the 2020–2021 season). Further, every player who has a higher career 3-point percentage than Bird has played in the NBA after he ended his career, with the vast majority playing since the turn of the millennia. Bird's 37.6% 3-point shooting was impressive in his day, but it pales in comparison to the success current players are having.[2]

Similarly, Magic Johnson, arguably the greatest point guard of all time, made only 325 3-pointers in his illustrious 13-year career, while hitting just over 30% of his attempts. And in the 1982–1983 season, Magic played 79 of 82 regular season games, yet made zero 3-pointers, missing all 21 of his attempts.[3] Conversely, in the first 10 years of Stephen Curry's career, he made almost 2,500 3-pointers and averaged 43.6%. And in the 2015–2016 season, Curry made 402 3-point shots. In one season, Curry made more 3-pointers than Magic did in his entire career.[4]

This is hard for many people to accept, especially with the folklore that surrounds these legendary athletes. But the truth remains, the game has changed and the players in the NBA are more talented shooting long range than players who played in the league in the past.

The Warriors were ahead of the curve with this and recognized they could transform the way they approached the game in order to build a champion. Rather than conforming to what had always been done, they discovered they could be more efficient by pulling their center and power forward out of the lane and having an offense that relied more on spacing, motion, and long-range shooting than grit, power, and low-post play. This led to an extraordinary surge in scoring (and success).

The same concept is true in business today. In order to succeed, you must stop denying the truth. Regardless of what you have done in the past, what your business model looked like, and where you placed your time, talents, and resources, you must recalibrate. The business world has transformed, so while the success you had previously may have been good, it will not generate the same results in this day and age.

Your products and services, tools and techniques, and approaches toward attracting and retaining customers must change. Every industry and market has transformed. This requires every business to make pivotal changes as well. The ability to rest on the laurels of past successes and opportunity to deny the truth is gone. To continue winning, you must embrace the new, dynamic business environment that is present throughout the world.

LET GO OF THE PAST

The Golden State Warriors changed the way basketball is played. Rather than conforming to what had always been done, the Warriors discovered they could be more efficient by transforming how their offense operated.

Not surprisingly, this dynamic transformation was more than what many traditional basketball experts could comprehend, especially in the beginning. Centers and power forwards scoring in the low post had always been critical for basketball teams. So, pulling them out of the lane was a complete transformation for how the game was played, and beyond what many experts would accept. Many analysts proclaimed the Warriors would never be successful because they didn't possess the strengths the team needed to win. Even after their first championship, people who had been around the NBA for their entire lives were still calling their success a fluke; their style of play was not sustainable.

For the overwhelming majority, the rationale behind their unwillingness to buy into Golden State's run was encapsulated in the overwhelming inability to think outside the box and a sincere belief that they knew better. Exuding confidence is a great characteristic traditionally, but failing to maintain a grasp on reality and accepting the changes that are occurring all around you can be devastating and has the potential for great organizations to miss out on the opportunity to deliver consistent results.

This aligns closely with the *Dunning–Kruger Effect*. The Dunning–Kruger Effect is a cognitive bias in which people of limited knowledge or ability inaccurately believe they have superior talents and/or wisdom. This lack of self-awareness causes considerable challenges because these people cannot objectively evaluate their competence.

This is what occurred in the NBA during the beginning of the Warriors amazing run. Unwilling to accept that the increased talent level of players would cause the game to change, so-called "experts" would not acknowledge the need for teams to adapt their style of play.

Bringing this to business, many struggling companies erroneously believe that they are above all of the changes that are affecting every industry and market in the world. Rather than modifying their approach, they quietly wait for the storm to pass. Though there have been tough years that caused struggles they did not anticipate, they believe that it will not last and their company will recover.

Much like how the Golden State Warriors changed the way basketball is played, so too has technology transformed the way every part of the business world operates. Technological advances breed new, innovative ways to streamline operations, optimize employee performance, and delight customers. Yet for all of the benefits that have materialized because of the digital age, many companies still choose to hold onto archaic methodologies and cumbersome approaches. They remain convinced they know better than what the market is telling them.

Whether you want to believe it or not, the transformations you are seeing in every industry and market make it clear that the world has changed, and you need to change as well. Traditional business models that yielded positive results in the past will not produce the same outcomes in the future. In order to keep up with the ultracompetitive global market, you must constantly be on offense and always look for ways to advance and improve.

TRUST IN YOUR DATA

Baseball has been using advanced analysis of data since the turn of the millennia. Rigorous analysis has helped teams identify how to approach unique situations based on advanced study of calculations and probability.

Basketball was slower to adopt. While data was used in certain scenarios, outside of rudimentary analysis, teams didn't dive deep into data. This is where Golden State found an opportunity. Analyzing different sets of data and actions taken by players on the court, top brass at Golden State found that NBA players had almost the exact same success rate shooting the ball from 23 feet away from the basket as they did from 24 feet. You wouldn't necessarily think this was a big deal, but the 3-point line is 23 feet and 9 inches away from the basket.

That meant that while the success rates of the shots taken were almost identical, the value for each basket was different. This created a huge disparity in the ROI for each shot taken. The ROI of a 2-point shot from 23 feet away yielded only 0.76 points whereas the ROI of a 3-point shot was 1.09 points, a 43% increase.

This created a quantifiable rationale for players to avoid long 2-point shots and place emphasis on shooting 3-pointers. It also opened the door for a new way to beat the competition. This cutting-edge information coupled with the dynamic long-range ability of Stephen Curry, Klay Thompson, and others on the team created a huge advantage for the Warriors. In the 2014–2015 season, the team took almost 11% more 3-pointers than they did the previous year, and then 14% more the following year. They also made a higher percentage than anyone in the league during both seasons.

This aligns closely with the way transformative businesses are taking control of their future. It is no secret that competition is fiercer than ever, so the importance of making calculated decisions based on quality data is imperative and consistently opens the door to increased financial gains.[5]

TAKE YOUR SHOT

For as brazen as the Warriors were, there is one undeniable truth – their plan could have failed.

The team could have gone all in on their new strategy and fell flat on their face. This is not an appealing outlook, but it is reality. Their strategy could have resulted in painfully embarrassing seasons that left everyone scratching their heads as to why they tried this inconceivable approach.

Yet the Golden State Warriors were undeterred.

This is primarily because they knew that if they remained the same, they would continue to be a below-average team that never had a chance of reaching their full potential, let alone win championships. As such, the risk of not changing posed an even bigger threat. They were sure to remain in obscurity, while other teams collected championship rings. Because of this, they pulled their center and power forward out of the lane, built an offense focused on ball movement, spacing, and the 3-point shot, and began systematically destroying everyone in the league.

An unwillingness to change can be for a variety of reasons, but a common factor is often the fear of failure. What if the change doesn't work? What if you make the wrong decision? What if the actions you take cause you to lose millions of dollars?

These are all legitimate concerns, but they pale in comparison to what *will* happen if you do not change – certain death.

The Golden State Warriors knew this, so they took action. However, they were not without flaws or missteps. They brought in players that did not fit into their system, designed plays that did not work, and experimented with lineups that were unsuccessful. These failures are not remembered by many people. This is because the team continued to adapt and evolve while trying new things.

This is similar to what many industry leaders have gone through. Most people do not remember the painful missteps of Google launching Google+, when Netflix spun off DVD sales into a new company called Qwikster, or when Steve Jobs was fired by Apple. This is because these exceptional organizations do not fear failure. Instead, they take action, build on their successes, and learn from their mistakes. This enables them to constantly adapt, evolve, and improve.

Those unwilling to make change will inevitably lose. This is exacerbated by how quickly change materializes in today's environment and is a primary reason so many old, traditional, industry-leading companies are failing in today's market. The exceptionally fast pace that change is occurring scares companies (and leaders) into resisting. Instead of embracing the unique way businesses can now serve customers, improve operations, and engage employees, leaders hold onto age-old practices that worked in the past, yet fail to have relevance in today's market. This conservative approach causes them to fall behind their competition and to become insignificant.

It is understandable to resist change because of the fear of failure, but value is lost when other organizations are willing to push forward and you choose to be stagnant. Resisting change paralyzes your business. Progress cannot occur if you are merely treading water, especially when all of your competition is being swept up by a powerful current that is aggressively heading toward the prize.

If you resist change, your company will navigate down a predictable path that ends in disappointment. Negative results from the resistance to change are not likely to be immediate or dramatic, but not modifying your business to meet what the market demands will eliminate your ability to compete in the long run. Even if you are already succeeding in your market, the need to constantly adapt, evolve, and improve is present.

The Golden State Warriors understood this when they replaced Head Coach Mark Jackson for Steve Kerr. They were already moving in the right direction, but they knew to get to the next level, they needed to make a move. To be fair, this seemed counterintuitive to most. Having just had one of their most successful seasons in the past 4 decades, there was fairly limited rationale for why they would want to make such a big move. Most of the players actually balked at the idea of a coaching change. The team had a budding superstar in Stephen Curry, talented role players, and a coach that seemed to be getting the best out of his team. Nevertheless, they still pulled the trigger. Shortly after they did, everyone understood why.

Sadly, many companies fail to maintain this open perspective, especially when they are succeeding. Organizations become nostalgic about past successes or fight change for interest in maintaining a seemingly easier path. Rather than proactively identifying the best opportunities to improve while simultaneously executing a forward-leaning plan, they hold onto past glory. This will only cause harm down the line.

Every product and service has a shelf life, and in most circumstances, it is much shorter than anticipated. This is evident with the Golden State Warriors. The Warriors made it to the NBA Finals 5 straight seasons from 2015 to 2019 and won three NBA Championships. However, in the 2019–2020 season, they had the worst record in the league. The polarizing team that took the world by storm dropped to the bottom of the league in the blink of an eye. Though injuries, free agency, and players no longer being as effective as they used to be have gone into this collapse, this drop in success displays the unique plunge that can happen to even the best organizations.

Competitors will copy you and challengers will find ways to make your current products and services obsolete. This necessitates that you take your shot when you have it. You never know how long you will have until your window of opportunity closes.

ADAPT, EVOLVE, AND IMPROVE

When the Golden State Warriors started making their impressive run, they already had good players. However, there was something missing. They didn't have the makeup of a group that would settle into a traditional NBA roster, nor did all of their players have talents that would blend well with one another. This required the team to assess the talents of each member of their squad, determine how they could change to deliver maximum value, and execute the best course of action to make that happen. They did this by creating a new way of playing basketball. This ultimately led to numerous championships while simultaneously revolutionizing the game!

Yet throughout the entire process, their seemingly unconventional decision-making was questioned by many traditionalists voicing opposition to their approach. These basketball analysts highlighted Golden State's unwillingness to fall in line with the way basketball had always been played and the importance of not just being a team that could shoot from the outside.

They didn't listen. They knew they needed to change to be successful.

This is similar to the way transformational businesses operate. They do not romanticize glory days and hold onto what was successful in the past, while rolling their eyes at the transformation that is taking place all around them. They modify their business and adjust to the "new normal" that is required to succeed.

The volatility of the market and changes in every industry in the world make it necessary that you constantly adapt, evolve, and improve. Five years prior to the fall of Blockbuster, Toys "R" Us, and Borders Bookstore, who would have predicted the wheels would have fallen off so quickly? And what could have been salvaged if the companies reacted to the changes in their industry faster? These questions have become obsolete for these former giants, but they could not be more important for your organization today. Do not rest on your laurels of past success; it will end up costing you in the long run. Instead, take action. Adapt, evolve, and improve.

BRINGING IT ALL TOGETHER

The Golden State Warriors did many things right over the course of the past decade, yet the primary reason they were able to win championships was that they brought a culture of change with them. They knew that competing the old way would not enable them to win. Their skillset didn't align with how other teams played and they would not be able to leverage the unique talents they had. While this change would have been difficult for most teams, it was simple for the Warriors. They understood their abilities would only be able to shine if they transformed the way they played.

This is the same for businesses today. The old path to success is gone. In order to win in today's economy, you must adapt, evolve, and improve. No company is safe from the extraordinary changes that are taking place, and just because you produced quality results in the past does not mean it will translate into consistent success in the future. In order to win moving forward, you must change and execute.

NOTES

1. Team Rankings. "NBA Team Three Pointers Attempted Per Game." *TeamRankings.com*. www.teamrankings.com/nba/stat/three-pointers-attempted-per-game (accessed April 8, 2020).
2. Basketball Reference. "NBA & ABA Career Leaders and Records for 3-Pt Field Goal Pct." *Basketball-Reference.com*. www.basketball-reference.com/leaders/fg3_pct_career.html (accessed April 8, 2020).

3. ESPN. "Magic Johnson." *ESPN.com.* www.espn.com/nba/player/stats/_/id/2334/ magic-johnson (accessed March 15, 2020).

4. ESPN. "Stephen Curry." *ESPN.com.* www.espn.com/nba/player/stats/_/id/3975/ stephen-curry (accessed March 15, 2020).

5. Cohen, Ben. "The Golden State Warriors Have Revolutionized Basketball." *WSJ. com.* www.wsj.com/articles/the-golden-state-warriors-have-revolutionized-bas ketball-1459956975 (accessed May 1, 2020).

Section III

Inside Your Organization

It is evident changes in the business world have transformed the marketplace and the external environment that we all compete in. However, the internal structure is also evolving. This requires leaders, employees, and the internal workings of every organization to adapt and evolve, knowing that it is not just about the organization changing directions externally but also about the importance of how everything on the inside functions.

Specifically, leaders must incorporate new attributes and traits to successfully bring out the best in workers. Employees must adopt a fresh methodology and a different set of skills to advance in their careers. Companies must identify cutting-edge operational activities and tactical procedures to give them an advantage over their counterparts.

Focusing on the four core questions when reading this section, it is important to understand how the internal workings of an organization have changed and will continue to change. However, rather than just focusing on the four core questions related to how it will affect your company, department, or team, in this section it is necessary to assess them from the perspective of an individual as well. This will enable you to identify the specific actions you need to personally take to put yourself in the best position to expand your influence, increase the value you provide, and bolster your career. Because just as the external environment has transformed in recent years, so too has the internal operation of each business changed. As such, while reading this section, place emphasis on identifying how you can personally change to improve yourself and your organization from the inside.

- What do you do?
- What could make you obsolete or replaceable?
- What change can you make to eliminate this risk?
- What specific actions can you take to execute this change?

In this section, there are seven specific actions leaders, employees, and companies must leverage to be viable over the next 10 years. These actions are not all-encompassing, though do properly highlight critical measures that must be implemented to flourish.

7

Leaders

The role of a leader has always been challenging. Leaders are directly accountable for the success or failure of an organization, department, or team. This responsibility will always be the most important part of their job.

However, while a leader's overarching responsibility has not changed, the way they fulfill their role has. This is because the knowledge, skills, and abilities leaders need to be successful have changed because of the way the workplace has evolved. While leaders will inevitably need different qualities and characteristics, depending on their industry, function, and job level, there are seven important behaviors all leaders will need over the next decade to be successful.

Specifically, in today's environment, leaders must:

- Leverage cross-functional collaboration to solve dynamic problems
- Be comfortable sharing decision-making responsibilities
- Be open to communication changes
- Demonstrate integrity and maintain emotional discipline
- Be serial masters continually developing expertise across domains
- Implement agile execution based on rapid iteration
- Be technologically savvy and have an interest in pushing innovation

It is critical that leaders leverage these behaviors to optimize the value their organization delivers. Below is more detailed information about the seven behaviors and the rationale as to why they will be so valuable moving forward.

LEVERAGE CROSS-FUNCTIONAL COLLABORATION TO SOLVE DYNAMIC PROBLEMS

Business silos involve departments working completely independent from one another, creating major barriers to communication, innovation, and productivity. When companies have business silos, information is only shared on a need-to-know basis. This degrades the overall vitality of an organization and reduces productivity and employee morale. Leaders who have business silos place a priority on department and team goals over company objectives and large-scale initiatives.

Business silos were a common practice many years ago, and companies could typically function adequately with them. This is no longer true in today's economy. The complexity of the workplace and matrixed environment that is now commonplace in almost every organization requires you to be able to merge resources and collaborate with other departments to be effective. Cross-functional collaboration creates synergies and produces collective success that ultimately generates competitive advantage, while simultaneously eliminating unnecessary work and excessive lag time.

Yet there are still some leaders who believe business silos are practical. They don't like the way collaboration and integration make work more intricate. They prefer to have their operation run without interference. Similarly, some leaders pride themselves on holding onto information and only sharing when it is absolutely necessary. They don't want to let go of the hold they have on their department, because they believe they will suddenly lose power (and control) if they do. Both of these types of leaders will invariably produce worse results than those who are capable of leveraging cross-functional collaboration. The world is too complex to maintain this archaic management style. To have an effective organization, leaders must be able to bring employees together and blend talents effectively.

Moving forward, all products, services, tools, technologies, lines of business, departments, teams, clients, and colleagues are going to become increasingly integrated, making it necessary to be able to leverage synergies and employ dynamic solutions to complex problems. Knowing how to get things done through formal and informal channels across the organization is paramount. Leaders who can collaborate with others and make timely, well-informed decisions to achieve collective goals will successfully advance organizational priorities, capitalize on new opportunities, and resolve problems quicker and more efficiently. They will also be lauded by their organization. Those who cannot do this will inevitably fade into obscurity.

BE COMFORTABLE SHARING DECISION-MAKING RESPONSIBILITIES

Many leaders have a chronic unwillingness to empower employees. They possess an inherent interest in making every decision while growing increasingly overwhelmed and less productive. Rather than delegate responsibilities or ask for help, these leaders lash out at subordinates with urgent requests and immediate demands, causing them to become further isolated. This results in their inability to balance their day and manage those around them and creates a tidal wave of chaos.

For those with this mentality, stop making excuses. Stop saying leaders have more responsibilities than they did in years past. And stop justifying your actions with faulty logic. The only thing you are doing is enabling your poor performance and the inability for your team to function optimally.

As a leader, you will often command the most airtime. That does not mean you need to have all the answers or the most expertise. Stop replacing competence with authority. Have the self-awareness to leverage your strengths and understand your shortcomings. This will maximize the value you and your team will produce, while minimizing unnecessary lag time and duplication of effort.

Businesses are too complex and there is too much going on to maintain control of everything. Leaders at every level have an increased number of responsibilities to execute, platforms to master, and procedures that must be followed. This causes them to not have the bandwidth to complete every project or fulfill every task without entrusting others with decision-making responsibilities. Not surprisingly, many leaders do not enjoy sharing decision-making responsibilities. However, if done properly, it can be a force multiplier that improves productivity and frees up the leader's time.

Further, by entrusting employees with decision-making authority, workers are not merely waiting for leaders to tell them to perform their role, but rather, taking ownership of responsibilities. This sense of ownership instills freedom that elevates performance. It pushes employees away from apathy and toward an interest in performing their best, enabling companies to transform from a business with managers and subordinates to an organization filled with leaders at every level. This inevitably provides employees independence and opens the door to increased innovation, creativity, and efficiency.

In this day and age, this is beyond critical. In a world that is filled with jobs that require more decisions to be made and difficult tasks to be completed, the importance of having employees capable of making real-time decisions is essential. The exceptional workload that leaders must balance and unique complexities that every industry now has make it no longer an option to empower and delegate, but rather, a necessity.

It will always be important to maintain a strong presence, but that is only part of the equation. Because, while leaders impress employees by showcasing their strengths, they change them by helping them develop. By sharing decision-making responsibilities, you will have a group of dedicated employees growing their skills while simultaneously being committed to producing optimal results.

BE OPEN TO COMMUNICATION CHANGES

In the past, communication between leaders and employees traditionally occurred through rudimentary methods that involved structured interaction in which the leader was the predominant person sharing information. This is no longer the case.

Communication between leaders and employees has transformed in every way possible, including who communicates, what is communicated, the types of communication mediums used, and how often leaders and employees communicate. This is primarily because every business is busier, more complex, and facing more unique challenges than ever before.

The complexity of every role in every organization in every industry has increased. Employees now possess expertise in their domain that extends far beyond the days of old when mechanical skill and manual labor were the primary areas of importance. In truth, employees have never been more skilled or educated than now, providing them tacit abilities that often extend well beyond what leaders possess. This makes them more prepared to engage in intelligent discussions that are focused on decision-making instead of blindly following orders. This openness leverages employees' talents and maximizes their output. Because of this, leaders are expected to have a conversation when engaging employees, not give a monologue.

Additionally, sharing information and communicating as a whole has increased in every facet of life, making it no surprise that leaders and employees would communicate more. Social media, smartphones, and constant contact with virtually anyone at any time have instilled a deep desire to know everything that is going on, at all times. This interest is now instinctive, including in the workplace. Employees want to know everything that is happening in their organization.

Similarly, the mechanism used to communicate in the workplace is constantly evolving. From communicating through word of mouth and mailing letters, to landlines and emails, all the way to instant messages and virtual reality, the platform for how information is shared never remains constant. Face-to-face interaction and verbal communication will never be eliminated completely, but high-tech alternatives are becoming increasingly important due to their practicality. Expanded workloads, increased travel demands, and alternative schedules make the use of technological resources no longer an option, but a necessity. Many people are not innately drawn to communicating by way of advanced technology. However, a large proportion of employees in the work environment, including younger generations, now prefer these methods. While your preference should be acknowledged, it is not the only opinion that matters. How employees desire to communicate must be equally valued. Be open to alternatives.

Finally, the increased frequency of communication is also important due to the complexity of the work that is being done. A lot of jobs that involve the use of mechanical skills are being replaced by professions that require cognitive abilities. Dynamic decision-making now plays a large part in almost every occupation in the market. This makes it no longer just about pushing a button, pulling a lever, or moving something from Point A to Point B. Instead, deductive reasoning and critical thinking skills must be applied in real time, and this requires more consistent communication.

The importance of being adaptable when communicating with employees will be essential over the next 10 years. The advances in technology, the increase in employee skill level, and the unique thirst people have for sharing and receiving information make it no surprise that changes in communication are necessary. Take heed and transform your mentality for how you plan to communicate to meet the new demands of the workforce.

DEMONSTRATE INTEGRITY AND MAINTAIN EMOTIONAL DISCIPLINE

Every leader will either be a great example or a terrible warning. This requires you to be careful with how you choose to lead. Regardless of what you want to believe and what you think is fair, everything you do as a leader is watched. The words you speak, the actions you take, and the way you conduct yourself in and out of the workplace are more scrutinized than ever, and if you fail to demonstrate integrity and maintain emotional discipline, your employees will want nothing to do with you.

This has always been the case, but it is more important in today's business climate because of the incredible shift in power that has taken place over the past 2 decades. When employees recognize a leader's lack of character, it will cause them to lose respect for the leader, while simultaneously triggering them to become less inclined to put forth any significant effort. Employees look at leaders as a source of inspiration, feed off of their energy, and count on them to be strong. Additionally, they typically align their actions and behaviors with the way their leader behaves.

Actions such as emotional outbursts, failing to take accountability, and taking advantage of the power (and privilege) your role provides are all shortcomings that drive employees away. Though you may not believe these actions are important, perpetually missing the mark is always recognized by employees and creates a chasm that builds over time.

This has the potential to rock the very foundation of a leader's relationship with his or her employees, while simultaneously causing the employees to reduce their ethical compass as well. This is no surprise, but the catastrophic effects of making mistakes today are magnified due to the way information is disseminated through organizations (and the world). Employees have a louder voice and more power than ever before. With seemingly everyone holding onto devices capable of sharing valuable information everywhere they go, the ability to highlight a leader's failure to demonstrate integrity or maintain emotional discipline can be distributed quickly and easily, causing an otherwise stellar career to crumble almost immediately.

This has been seen time and again by way of an unethical decision made by a prominent business leader, a self-focused action taken by a politician, and an ill-advised choice carried out by a police officer. While an individual could have demonstrated integrity and maintained emotional discipline for his or her entire career, a single indiscretion could destroy an otherwise clean record.

With the incredible speed at which change occurs, challenges arise, and markets fluctuate, the importance of being able to face adversity and remaining resolute and forthright cannot be overstated. This necessitates that a leader always demonstrates integrity and maintains emotional discipline.

BE SERIAL MASTERS CONTINUALLY DEVELOPING EXPERTISE ACROSS DOMAINS

The days of settling in and resting on the skills you have obtained are gone. The world is moving too fast to accept this anymore. The complex business environment and accelerated rate of change make it impossible to only have skills in one core area of business and expect to have sustained success. Quality leaders understand this and appreciate the importance of building talents outside of their current skillset. They know they must broaden their knowledgebase in order to meet new challenges and become more valued.

This can be done by expanding knowledge in your specific career field or crossing over to a new function and gaining insights into how other departments operate. Even something as simple as sitting with frontline employees to gain a better perspective on what they do each day will expand your skills and make you more capable of effectively leading your team.

Many leaders like to brush off the need to develop additional expertise, but the truth is, the skills acquired yesterday quite often fail to translate into the tools needed for tomorrow. In order to remain relevant, you must continue to invest in yourself.

Disappointingly, even with the extraordinary changes that are taking place in the business world, some leaders still believe they don't need to acquire additional talents because they are in a static industry or do nothing but manage employees. The notion that your responsibilities or business environment will not change is grossly inaccurate and lacks long-term vision. It is merely an excuse used to minimize the need to continue improving yourself. This will ultimately reduce the value you deliver to your company. Your knowledge, skills, and abilities will grow stale over time, resulting in you becoming less productive if you do not invest in yourself. Further, as new leaders join the ranks and continue to improve themselves, the lethargic approach you hold onto will cause you to become expendable.

If you truly want to have sustained success as a leader, you must continue investing in yourself by developing expertise across domains.

_____

IMPLEMENT AGILE EXECUTION BASED ON RAPID ITERATION

Speed to market and maintaining a consistent direction that comprises delivering value efficiently are wildly more important than creating a flawless plan. Yet leaders all over the world place emphasis on creating perfection over generating results, waiting to make decisions rather than choosing a course of action, and devoting exorbitant time and energy into activities that fail to move the needle instead of delivering value-add initiatives.

Stop wasting time trying to make things perfect; they will never be. Stop waiting to make a decision; you will never have all the information you want. Stop spending time on things that no one cares about; focus on projects that add value. We should all strive to make good decisions, produce quality work, and deliver excellence. However, creating a product or service that cannot be improved or developed more in the future is not realistic, so the delay in bringing it to market isn't practical. Business is moving too fast to accept delays. This means you will never have all the information you want, the decisions you make will always include some level of risk, and the longer you wait, the more danger you will be in.

Leaders must have a bias for action and be constantly leaning forward, with clear intent and focus on moving in a particular direction. There will inevitably be pivots that need to be made along the way, but leaders moving with a sense of purpose rather than waiting to choose a path will generate forward momentum. This will create the opportunity to make better decisions as progress is made.

In truth, the smallest action is better than the greatest of intention, and quite often, after initial action is taken, the next steps unveil themselves allowing more calculated decisions to be made based on the results of the initial action. In the extraordinarily complex business environment that we all live in, you must make decisions and continually iterate as you progress. This will enable you to add value to the organization while constantly fine-tuning your deliverables.

To be successful you must be able to make quality decisions and pivot based on what you discover. Implement agile execution based on rapid iteration.

EMBRACE TECHNOLOGY AND USE INNOVATION

Complacency breeds comfort and comfort leads to extinction. Leaders that don't understand this will be out of a job soon. No company, department, or team can remain the same and expect to have sustained success. Instead, they will lose relevance and become obsolete.

This is evident from the way jobs in certain industries disappear. How critical are Bank Tellers? Receptionists? And Travel Agents? All of them were important at one point in time, but their level of usefulness has become almost nonexistent in recent years. This begs the question, at what point will their utility be phased out completely? And how many other jobs, teams, departments, and companies will have this same fate become their reality?

This is happening throughout the world. Every part of every business in every industry and market must constantly adapt and evolve to remain relevant and meet the new demands of customers. This necessitates the willingness to embrace technology and use innovation whenever possible. Yet many leaders don't want to accept this, choosing instead to erroneously believe their space within their organization and industry will not change, regardless of the situation. This perspective is shortsighted.

Technological advances and improvements in innovation constantly disrupt industries and naturally affect the flow of business, creating the need for people to change. This eliminates the idea that you can put technology and innovation on the back burner and expect to build sustained success. Even everyday tasks like meetings, sharing information, and training classes rely heavily on advances in technology and innovation.

This makes it clear that you must embrace technology and bring it into every possible part of organizational life. Technology and innovation are continually becoming more integrated into our world. To remain relevant, leaders must be willing to break from their routine and discover what technologies and innovations they can use to optimize workplace performance.

BRINGING IT ALL TOGETHER

Leaders will inevitably need different talents, abilities, and skills dependent on numerous variables, including the industry, market, function, and job level they are in. However, leveraging these seven overarching behaviors will enhance the productivity of you and your staff, regardless of what position you are in. Successfully incorporating these behaviors will lead to expanding your influence, increasing the value you generate for your company, and improving the results you and your team deliver. Embrace them, because just as businesses are unable to succeed if they do not evolve, so too do leaders grow stale if they do not adapt to the everchanging needs of the business world.

8

Employees

Retail store managers, jobs in manufacturing, and librarians were all once sought-after professions that had job security, quality benefits, and dependable futures. That is far from true today. Online shopping, automation in manufacturing, and e-books now make these once secure career paths unstable. People can still have success with these careers, but the severe drop in demand for these jobs make it clear – going into one of these professions is not advisable.

Industries, markets, and workplaces are constantly evolving, making it necessary that employees transform as well. Certain characteristics that were once valuable have less relevance now. This, in a nutshell, captures the true challenge people face in the workplace today. The unique transformations that are occurring in industries and markets throughout the world make it difficult for employees to know how to build a successful career.

To remain aligned with the transformations that are taking place, employees must adapt and evolve. Below are seven key actions employees must embrace to build a successful career over the next decade:

- Become a specialist by developing highly coveted skills
- Never stop learning
- Be flexible, careers are not linear
- Build your living resume
- Surround yourself with greatness
- Be easy to work with
- Increase your technological prowess

BECOME A SPECIALIST BY DEVELOPING HIGHLY COVETED SKILLS

Being a generalist and having a wide breadth of knowledge in any field, industry, or business is important. The ability to understand various areas within an ecosystem, company, or department enables you to walk into any environment and be comfortable. But this alone will not enable you to have success. Instead, you will plateau. In order to have sustained success, you must have a particular set of skills that are of significant value to an organization.

This is true for a variety of reasons, but primarily because of the extraordinary competition that exists in every industry and market in the world. The global economy is fierce, with margins being slimmer and competition becoming more intense than ever before. No organization stands alone when creating new products and services. No department works independent from the rest of the company. And no employee operates without support from others on their team. Instead, everything is woven together, with the cream of the crop rising to the top.

If you are adequate at everything but fail to excel at anything, how will your skills be used? What value will you bring to your department? How will you help your company succeed?

Specialization breeds competitive advantage and is the gateway to establishing yourself as a formidable employee. It is always beneficial to have a wide array of talents, but specialization sets people apart. For example, the nurse who excels in urgent care, salesman who knows just what to say to close the deal, and IT whiz who can create a captivating website, all have unique skills that cause them to stand out from the crowd. Each will undoubtedly have other talents, but it is that one trait that makes them truly valuable. This is true across every industry and function in the business world.

There are many ways you can become a specialist, but the most important thing to do involves dedicating time and energy into developing your craft. Elaborate planning and philosophical discussion do nothing to help you advance in your journey. Immerse yourself in what you are passionate about and incessantly work toward improving in areas that are valued. Put in the hours, days, weeks, months, and years it will take to truly become an expert. Doctors spend almost a decade in school to earn their title.

Olympians devote their lives to perfecting their craft. Musicians practice late into the night to earn their stripes. To be a specialist, you need to do the same.

It will always be important to have well-rounded skills, but those who have crafted a unique talent will fare much better. So, while it is great your grandfather was a generalist who had a variety of talents that enabled him to get ahead in his career, we are living in a different era; it is no longer as important to be a jack of all trades. Rather than just maintaining a broad knowledgebase, hone your skills to be exceptional in one particular area. This will create a competitive advantage and allow you to differentiate yourself from others.

NEVER STOP LEARNING

In 1940, 24% of adults, 25 years or older, had their high school diploma and 4.6% had a bachelor's degree or higher in the United States. In 1970, 50% of adults, 25 years or older, had their high school diploma and 11% had a bachelor's degree or higher. And in 2000, 80% of adults, 25 years or older, had a high school diploma, 25% had a bachelor's degree, and 8.9% had an advanced degree.[1]

In short, having a diploma in the 1940s separated you from your counterparts. In the 1970s, a college degree created distance between you and other employees. And in 2000, a graduate degree was the key for you to stand out among the crowd.

Yet, since the turn of the millennia, the tide has turned again, with the bar being raised to an even higher standard. In 2018, 90% of adults, 25 years or older, have a high school diploma, 35% have a bachelor's degree, and 13% have an advanced degree.[2]

This makes it clear, while formal education used to be a powerful differentiator, it is no longer enough. The business world is now filled with employees who have formal education and expertise at higher levels than ever before. So, while earning a degree may be mandatory in some fields, it no longer sets you apart, nor does it carry as much weight as it once did.

What is more important are unique skills that enable you to succeed in the dynamically changing business environment and the ability to apply what you learn on the job. Continually advancing your skills so that you can keep up with the changing tides of the business world is where people truly set themselves apart. With technological innovations, business practices, and societal trends transforming quickly and consistently, often without notice, you cannot afford to rest on your laurels and bask in what you have already accomplished. Formal education is still important, but it pales in comparison to being able to increase your knowledgebase so that you are able to continually increase the value you deliver to your company. This is particularly because a lot of what you will need to know and do to be successful wasn't taught (or necessarily even invented) when you were in school.

Resist the urge to rely on your degree, certification, or trade and place emphasis on building on these previously learned skills and abilities instead. The talents you developed in the past are not as desirable in the future due to the changes that are taking place today. Because of this, you must be a lifelong learner.

However, do not just place emphasis on formal education. Be open to how you advance your skills. In the past, formal education was a primary way to advance one's career, but this is no longer the case. Today, 70% of learning materializes from new and challenging experiences, 20% comes from communities, networks, and coaching, and 10% takes place from formal learning. Formal education is still important, but you cannot stop there. The world is moving too fast and changing too rapidly. Advances in technology, innovative techniques that streamline operations, and cutting-edge research that shifts industries require advancing your skills and fine-tuning your abilities through various mediums.

Because, while you may have gone to a good school and been privileged to get a quality education, that is not enough anymore. You must continue pushing forward, developing new talents, and expanding your knowledge. You must never stop learning.

BE FLEXIBLE: CAREERS ARE NOT LINEAR

In 1940, a young man named Edward, just shy of his 21st birthday, got a job as a Janitor's Assistant at a hydraulics plant in Southeast Michigan. As a dedicated employee committed to producing results, Edward worked at the company for 39 years, slowly climbing the ranks before retiring as the Chief Product Planning Engineer. There were many bumps along the road and important decisions he needed to make, but overall, Edward's career progression was quite linear. He continually took on increased responsibility with very few bends along the road. He would come into a new position, spend a couple of years working to master it, and then move on to the next level.

This career path was fairly typical back then. Employees would be able to predict their next move, when they would get a promotion, and how long they would have to wait to grow with the company. This still happens, but it is not as common today. The roadmap for employees in this day and age is far less linear than it was decades earlier. Complex business environments and changes in industries and markets create fluidity in the workplace, making career paths look very different than what was once deemed normal.

Because of this, you must be open to opportunities that might look different than what you would have expected. Specifically, career growth that you would think is outside of your traditional path could be a great fit. By keeping an open mind, you may have opportunities that deliver captivating experiences and help you advance in your career.

For example, prior to launching VaynerMedia and being an NYT Best Selling Author, Gary Vaynerchuk ran his father's wine business. Long before joining the tech industry, Co-founder of Netflix, Reed Hastings sold vacuums. And previous to becoming the CEO of General Motors, Mary Barra took leadership roles in manufacturing, human resources, and product development. Each of these examples highlights the benefits of being flexible with your career and how fluidity can prepare you for big opportunities in the future.

Additionally, beyond just keeping an open mind about opportunities that you initially believe might not be suitable for you is the importance of appreciating how positions that weren't necessarily important in years past could become prominent and highly coveted in the future. For example, 30 years ago, the Chief Technology Officer in a firm was rarely seen as a critical part of an organization. Though they served a valuable purpose in the company, they were primarily there just to make sure computers functioned properly. Today, they are a pivotal component of every company's strategy and day-to-day operation.

Similarly, 15 years ago, social media was in its infancy, with no one truly understanding what value it could generate. For the most part, social media was no more than a sidebar to the marketing manager's role. Now, many companies have social media teams and place emphasis on advancing their digital brand by investing considerable time and resources.

A linear path for career growth is still viable, but it is not the only route. Complex business environments enable employees to develop their skills in numerous ways. Being flexible and adaptable opens the door to potential opportunities while enabling you to develop your skills and build the career you want.

BUILD YOUR LIVING RESUME

Everyone in the workplace has a resume. Traditionally, resumes are a snapshot of what you have accomplished in your career, a look into what your skills are, and an example of what a company can expect you to achieve. And for the most part, they are only important during the select time you are trying to get a job.

Traditional resumes do a fine job sharing *what* you have done, but they only tell part of the story; your living resume shares the rest by explaining *how* you have done it. Your living resume shows how you perform your role, live your life, and act outside of the workplace. It represents how you treat people, honor your commitments, and fulfill your responsibilities. It is at its very essence, a true reflection of yourself and the values you hold dear in your life. And different than your traditional resume, which is only seen at certain times during your career, your living resume is on display all the time.

This is especially true today because of how much smaller the world has gotten. The opportunity to connect with others, from both near and far, has never been easier. This means your reputation has an easier time following you around, for better or worse. So, if you are out partying every night, involved in illicit relationships that do not serve you or others well, or are constantly involved in unnecessary drama, it will stick with you.

While it is not always acknowledged (or necessarily legal), employers factor in personal lives when hiring and promoting employees. What you put on your traditional resume is important. However, the actions you take every day are keystrokes into your living resume and often tell a more compelling story.[3] This makes it important to always put forth your best self.

Digging deeper, beyond just examples that occur out in the real world are the digital stories that we all tell. Access to information is at every person's fingertips, with employers, recruiters, and colleagues having the opportunity to learn about you, often without your knowledge. The ability to "Google someone" to learn about them is a practice that has become increasingly popular. Typically, results from these searches are benign, but there is the potential for unscrupulous behavior to result in negative consequences.

We have all seen morally bankrupt posts on social media, illicit videos on YouTube, and stories of inappropriate behavior on news sites. These actions immediately shape the perspective of how we view people and have the potential to destroy otherwise promising careers. Though one action shouldn't necessarily be an indictment on the person, it almost always follows them around wherever they go. To minimize this risk, you must place importance on maintaining a quality reputation both in and out of the workplace.

Traditional resumes will continue to be a primary source of truth. However, living resumes are growing more formidable. As everyone continues to grow more intertwined and the internet continues to become more involved in our lives, everything you do in every facet of your life will become more pertinent, documented, and analyzed. Make certain your living resume tells a compelling story that you will be proud to share.

SURROUND YOURSELF WITH GREATNESS

It has often been said that you are the average of your five closest friends. This should be no surprise. Spending a lot of time with people will often have you thinking, acting, and speaking like them. The same is true for who you spend time with at work. We all know certain people who push forward to reach great heights and become successful. We also know individuals who habitually fail to live up to expectations and have excuses for everything. Both types of employees can have considerable influence on your career, with it being no surprise that your success will often be directly correlated to theirs.

If you spend time with people who are making good choices and striving to deliver excellence in the workplace, they will inevitably bring you with them. Alternatively, if you surround yourself with those who habitually make ill-advised decisions and fail to reach their potential, your work will also suffer. This concept is not new or revolutionary, but it is valid.

When thinking about it holistically, would you really invest with a financial adviser who has no money? Take fitness advise from a personal trainer who is severely out of shape? Or follow the morality of an ethics professor who just got caught laundering money?

No, you wouldn't.

Then why would listen to the employee who isn't successful, yet has buckets of wisdom to share? Why hitch your wagon to the role model who can't stay out of trouble, yet has endless advice? Or why follow the individual who has been in the same job for numerous years, yet knows exactly what to do to get ahead?

If you want to achieve greatness, connect with those who are delivering value to the organization and pursuing excellence in everything they do. You will instinctively be more passionate about your career and more committed to achieving results.

Another benefit that comes with surrounding yourself with greatness is the increased amount of personal accountability you will develop. Almost without fail, those who achieve excellence maintain an extraordinary amount of personal accountability, whereas those who continue to underperform always have an excuse. This isn't new, but the gap between the two groups has grown considerably in recent years.

Instead of working to achieve greatness, many people surround themselves with enablers who passively accept excuses and validate mediocre performance. Rather than acknowledging less than exceptional productivity or pointing out an average routine, individuals surround themselves with people who indulge their innocuous behavior as stellar because it makes them feel good for the interim. It is comfortable. This ultimately lowers the bar and minimizes what is expected of you.

Having colleagues (and friends) who are supportive is important, but if you want to achieve success, it is necessary to have those closest to you be able to tell you that you need to step up your game. Trivial celebrations about activities that lack importance are placeholders for constructive criticism. They demean authentic success.

People who habitually cater to subpar performance do you no good. They enable you to sit comfortably where you are without actually growing, improving, or succeeding. This ultimately makes you expendable. Instead of buying into this farce, surround yourself with people who are authentic, will tell you the truth, and are constantly looking for ways to develop and improve. They will push you to new heights by challenging you to reach for greatness.

BE EASY TO WORK WITH

What do Cam Newton, Bryce Harper, and Russell Westbrook have in common?

All are supremely talented athletes with skills that have enabled them to compete at the highest level in their respective sports. Their raw talent and ability to rise to the occasion in seemingly the most intense situations have provided them the opportunity to reach a status very few athletes can ever get to.

They also possess characteristics that make them high maintenance and extremely difficult to work alongside. They have had behavioral issues with teammates, challenges with management, and outbursts that have caused their teams to suffer. Rather than lifting others up and bringing the best out of fellow players, they drag the team down and cause problems wherever they go. Opposite of a talent multiplier, they are toxic to their environment, with their supreme skills being the only reason their antics are accepted.

They will continue to have successful careers, but they will always be in the middle of controversy while jumping from organization to organization. This will likely prevent any of them from ever winning a championship. Instead, they will be in a constant state of chaos. You may be one to provide excuses for these players (and others like them), but the truth is, they lack the self-awareness necessary to acknowledge they are hurting themselves, the players around them, and their organization.

For employees who have these types of characteristics, you will be overlooked, not included, and habitually left out. In this day and age, the secret to success isn't having the most talent, being the most intelligent, or having the best title; it is about having a quality work ethic, being able to work well with others, and blending your skills with the skills of those around you. Talent has the potential to take you to the top, but it is the content of your character that will ultimately enable you to succeed. And in a world filled with amazingly capable people, organizations can easily trade out an employee who does not work well with others for an employee who does.[4]

You may believe this is unfair or unethical, but it actually aligns with every part of life. Do you want to spend time with friends who are easy to deal with and bring out the best in you or individuals who cause you frustrations and create anxiety? Do you go to the restaurant that is always a hassle to get in and has an incompetent staff or a venue with plenty of space and knowledgeable waiters and waitresses? And are you more apt to purchase a Blackberry phone that is clunky and hard to navigate or the latest iPhone/Android that is intuitive and easy to use?

These decisions are easy.

So are the ones that involve what type of colleagues you want to work alongside. There is no question, you are almost always hired for your skills and fired for your behavior. This means your commitment to character must be intact. If you are hard to work with, constantly making projects more difficult than they have to be, and unable to maintain positive relationships in the office, you are at risk.

This is especially true if the value you generate begins to decline. Though not always acknowledged, companies will often put up with self-serving, obnoxious, narcissists if they produce superior results. However, as soon as these problem employees stop delivering exceptional value, they are gone. And it is an easy decision. Conversely, employees who are easy to work with will almost always find a home in an organization, even if their productivity in their current role begins to dip. Quite often, instead of being laid off, they are reassigned to a new role.

Many companies express that employees are the most valuable resource in the organization, but that is only true when employees are performing their role and elevating the productivity of those around them. In order to do this, you must be easy to work with.

INCREASE YOUR TECHNOLOGICAL PROWESS

The shift toward knowledge-based, tech-focused roles has transformed the world and every business in it. Yet some people are still fighting the importance of being technologically savvy and choosing to believe that IT won't affect their industry, business, or role.

This could not be further from the truth.

Tech equals speed. Tech equals intellect. Tech equals money. And most importantly, tech equals options. Anyone who tells you tech isn't important will fall behind, and the massive gap between those who are willing to embrace technology and those who aren't is growing larger by the day.

Every company in every industry in every part of the world is leveraging new technology more and more, making it clear that technology-based skills are not just for a select few, but rather, important for everyone in the workplace. Everyone must increase their technological prowess and embrace new innovation to succeed in the future.

This is counterintuitive for many employees. When people think about IT, they quite often focus on a single element, rather than analyzing the various ways they can expand their skills. Coding, website development, and computer languages are important parts of the IT world, but there are other ways to build your skills as well.

Specifically, learning unique functions your computer program can perform, exploring ways to leverage analytics, automating manual tasks, and increasing your social media aptitude all fall under increasing your technological prowess. Even taking a Microsoft Excel class or watching videos on the internet exploring how to use data more effectively will serve you well.

In spite of these undeniable truths, there is still resistance due to the stigma that comes with IT. People believe that you are either technologically savvy or you are not. While individuals inevitably fall along a vast spectrum of talent levels, the notion that you are unable to develop your skills is merely an excuse not to try. People naturally develop where they invest their time and energy. In order to advance your skills, you must be willing to work on it.

It is undeniable that certain people have a stronger technological aptitude than others, but everyone can increase their skillset. And though your talents may not be extraordinary, even having a rudimentary level of technical ability is beneficial. Further, being tech savvy doesn't always mean you have to code or build websites. It could mean learning what technology can do to make your operation run more efficiently, how you can use it to analyze data better, and where you can incorporate it to speed up your process. Increasing your technological prowess means embracing ways to make the company you work for operate better by including technology, and it is the future of business.

BRINGING IT ALL TOGETHER

The role of an employee has evolved over time and will continue to change as the workplace changes. No one can maintain a stagnant approach and be successful. Instead, employees must align themselves with the changes that are occurring in the workplace and adapt to their continually evolving environment. Set yourself up for success by adopting these seven practices. By doing this, you will be preparing yourself for a long and successful career.

NOTES

1. United States Census. "Educational Attainment: 2000." Census.gov. https://www.census.gov/prod/2003pubs/c2kbr-24.pdf (accessed April 9, 2020).
2. United States Census. "Number of People with Master's and Doctoral Degrees Doubles Since 2000." *Census.gov.* www.census.gov/library/stories/2019/02/number-of-people-with-masters-and-phd-degrees-double-since-2000.html (accessed April 9, 2020).
3. Zern, Adam C. "Our Living Resume" (speech, DisruptHR, The Mezz, March 27, 2019).
4. Burke, Aaron. "The Character Test" (lecture, Radiant Church, Britton Plaza, September 8, 2019).

9

Policies, Processes, Procedures, and Performance

It is interesting to think about families who attend parties, especially during the holiday season. Certain families seem to have the process down to a science. Parents walk in with their children in tow, chat with other parents while their kids spend time with other children their age, and after three hours, the family departs for home with the parents saying that the kids need to get to bed or they will turn into little monsters. And rather than lingering at the party with dozens of goodbyes, countless hugs, and a seemingly endless barrage of last-minute discussions, the family quietly (and respectfully) slips out the door and heads for home. Any type of drama with the children is avoided, a long-standing conversation about unrelated topics is thwarted, and a slow, cumbersome walk to the car is evaded. Instead, the family seamlessly goes about their evening.

Alternatively, there are families who show up to parties that are a complete disaster. They get to the party late with one child in tears and the other obviously just recovering from a tantrum; an underlying sense of tension seems to follow them around, and they need a ton of support the entire time they are visiting. Plus, their departure is always a struggle. It takes 45 minutes to say goodbye to everyone at the get-together, as they haphazardly look for their children's shoes and blend long goodbyes with unnecessary discussion. And while the other family successfully timed their departure to coincide with when their children are at their best, this family seemingly waits for a catastrophic meltdown prior to leaving.

This aligns closely with how companies in the world function. Some organizations have a knack for optimizing productivity, developing products and services that are valuable to the market, and looking for ways to improve their operation. They know the results they want to achieve and execute the proper plan to get the job done.

Conversely, there are companies always on the verge of a breakdown, and though they want to be at the same level as the first company, they can't seem to get out of their own way. They have good intentions, but no real direction or identity. Though they say they are interested in making changes so they can improve, they are always involved in activities that are unrelated to their goals while consistently making things more difficult than necessary.

Companies predictably fall in between these polar opposites, and while there are no definitive answers for why some organizations thrive while others struggle, there are specific actions that enable some businesses to be successful while others wallow in obscurity. The following are seven areas of focus you must excel at over the next decade to be successful:

- Stop being process-focused, start being solutions-driven
- Stop glorifying busyness, start celebrating results
- Stop making work difficult, start delivering value
- Stop resisting progress, start updating and automating
- Stop celebrating mediocrity, start elevating performance
- Stop being unpredictable, start delivering consistency
- Stop accepting complacency, start being proactive

STOP BEING PROCESS-FOCUSED, START BEING SOLUTIONS-DRIVEN

UPS makes 18 million deliveries a day in the United States, requiring an extraordinary amount of coordination, collaboration, and commitment. The company is constantly embracing new technology, building better processes, and finding ways to make their operation more efficient. Yet, while they have exceptional leaders, top-notch talent, and state-of-the-art equipment to make their company flourish, one of the simplest ideas ever thought of transformed the company completely.

The idea – drivers should avoid left-hand turns unless absolutely necessary.

This practice shaves 185 million miles a year from their routes, eliminates emissions equivalent to over 20,000 cars, and saves between $300–$400 million annually in fuel alone. Additionally, due to left-hand turns being 10 times more likely to be a "critical pre-crash event" than right-hand turns, it also reduces the risk of motor vehicle accidents. The success of this practice has become so profitable, their routing software calculates the best possible route for each truck by favoring right-hand turns, sometimes going so far as to have drivers go around the block in favor of making a left.[1]

This is a perfect example of a company being solutions-driven instead of being consumed by developing an alluring process.

Bureaucratic red tape and emphasis on unnecessary procedures and activities that fail to generate value destroy productivity. Rather than being solutions-driven, companies put processes in place that drive people away from adding value and toward a state of frustration, all because they are looking to use a captivating way to complete the job instead of just focusing on delivering a valuable solution. For example, technology that is state-of-the-art yet does not enable employees to complete their role easily, projects that must be signed off by 11 vice presidents before being started, and virtual training that reaches a lot of people but does not help them understand the material all have a "check-the-box" mentality.

Though one could argue that processes are in place to ensure that chaos does not permeate throughout an organization, an excessive number of regulations that confines employees does not create order. Instead, it imposes on an employee's ability to fulfill their responsibilities.

Stop being process-focused. Start being solutions-driven.

The exceptionally complex business environment that we are now in requires a solutions-driven mentality. Excessive red tape and uniquely defined processes that create more complexities than necessary do not serve your organization well; they only make things more difficult. Excessive emphasis on process and following the rules pales in comparison to actually getting the job done. The only way you will be able to produce results to the level necessary to compete is to be solutions-driven.

STOP GLORIFYING BUSYNESS, START CELEBRATING RESULTS

A culture of busyness is not the key to success; it is the pathway to irrelevance, inefficiency, and failure.

A culture of busyness causes employees to find unrelated tasks to complete while not placing emphasis on activities that add value. A culture of busyness leads to an unfocused organization that lacks awareness of what it needs to do to be successful. And in many organizations today, a culture of busyness is seen as a badge of honor.

Having the opportunity to broadcast how much you have going on causes others to look at you with a level of admiration, while simultaneously pushing them to employ similar behavior. Everyone wants to be seen as someone who has endless responsibilities and is engaged with multiple activities. Yet quite often, it is unrelated to them producing results.

When looking at the situation from a different lens, what do these people actually accomplish? What value are they adding? Where have they improved the company? And most important, what is the reward for being involved in numerous endeavors versus actually producing results?

Many employees who are in constant motion are the most overrated associates in the organization because they fail to produce any tangible value. Being busy isn't necessarily a bad thing, but the inability to recognize what is important can be devastating.

Just like in sports, it isn't the team that is the busiest that wins, but rather, the one who produces the best results. For example, in basketball, it isn't the team that shoots the most shots that is the winner, but the one that scores the most points. In football, having more yards than the opposition can be valuable, but yards don't matter unless the team gets in the end zone. And in baseball, having more hits than the opposition is great, but if the hits don't translate into runs, they aren't worth anything.

The same is true in business. Instead of placing prominence on functional activities that generate monetary gain, we emphasize areas that lack relative importance yet keep people busy. It is great to be busy, but if busy doesn't create value, it doesn't matter.

Stop validating people who are the loudest in the room but produce the least. Stop commending those who consistently deliver sweeping declarations about what they are going to do, yet fail to create substantial value. And stop giving credit to individuals who provide rousing ideas yet never actually follow through. Action is more important than words and execution is better than ideas.

This seems straightforward, but it is continually lost on people and organizations. A lot of companies have employees operating under the belief that they need to be in a constant state of motion to be important and have witnessed many of their colleagues be rewarded according to this premise. So, meetings are scheduled for matters that could have been handled by email, people include themselves in projects when there is no viable reason for their involvement, and individuals prioritize extracurricular activities over traditional work for interest in bolstering their personal brand.

Rather than encouraging this inferior approach by continually glorifying workers who are busy, celebrate employees who produce results. Taking importance away from the incessant need to be in motion and replacing it with an emphasis on producing results creates a transformational change in the way business is performed. Colleagues will strive to execute at the highest levels instead of merely passing time by performing their responsibilities and hoping to be recognized by leaders. This shift highlights those who are making a difference and exposes employees who hide behind a mask of busyness.

To be successful, stop confusing the value of busyness and start placing emphasis on delivering results.

STOP MAKING WORK DIFFICULT, START DELIVERING VALUE

The saying "knowledge is power" has been around for decades and serves as a constant reminder that a critical component of success is understanding a certain subject, topic, or issue. The saying is catchy and seems to invoke a unique truth, but it is wrong. Knowledge is not power. Knowledge is merely awareness. Applied knowledge is power.

In order to actually deliver value to anything, you must take action! Bureaucratic processes, red tape, and convoluted procedures all fail to generate true value, yet plague companies throughout the world. Instead of committing to a course of action that will produce results, businesses place emphasis on elaborate activities that fail to generate anything tangible.

When you boil business down to the simplest form, every company is a system that needs to operate as quickly and efficiently as possible. This is not a novel concept. However, many companies still add barriers that restrict the ability for them to be successful.

This is especially true for companies that resist the urge to change and fight progressive techniques that could simplify operations. Rather than automating manual processes, finding ways to eliminate redundant activities, and removing programs that lack relevance, businesses justify their decisions based on the desire to not upset the flow of their operation. In theory this is attractive. However, the advanced state of the economy we are in makes it impractical. With extraordinary competition at every part of the value chain, the importance of removing unnecessary lag and excessive overprocessing is critical.

Making work more difficult than it has to be costs companies time and money, with the excess effort wasted, resulting in no additional value being generated. Whether it involves employees putting time and effort into procedures that are unnecessary or wasteful, equipment being used for misguided reasons, or a myriad of other avoidable actions, placing emphasis on activities that lack value pushes companies away from being competitive and toward a state of insignificance.

Further, beyond the monetary costs, making work more difficult than it has to be destroys morale. When employees experience a loss of productivity due to unnecessary activities being inserted into their daily routine, their inherent inclination is to reduce effort or remove themselves from their current work environment. Navigating around unnecessary obstacles is not appreciated by anyone. Most employees will begrudgingly complete the assignment, avoid putting forth their best effort, or look for a way out. Though this is not an attractive outlook, it is a natural response. Employees understand when their time and talents are being wasted and do not want to remain in that environment if they can avoid it.

Contrary to making work more difficult than it has to be is being obsessed with execution. Removing all unnecessary barriers and allowing employees to fulfill their duties without distraction or hindrance creates a unique motivation focused on delivering value. It is the way the best companies operate. They strip away all potential roadblocks and hindrances and prioritize delivering results.

If you want to be successful, stop making work more difficult than it has to be. Place all your efforts into getting things done. Even the best laid plans will require you to adjust as you go. Start moving forward and make changes as you progress.

STOP RESISTING PROGRESS, START UPDATING AND AUTOMATING

The world has changed, yet for some people, the interest in sticking with age-old processes and procedures is still strong. These people will tell you that it takes a little longer to do everything, but they get more satisfaction out of the hard work they put forth. They feel more accomplished putting in the extra time and effort to manually load the machine, run the report, or build the prototype. They like going the extra mile because it makes them feel like they are putting in an honest day's work.

This is not a sign of you being diligent and committed; it is a failure to understand what is important. Manual labor that could be done with automation shows your resistance to progress and lack of interest in building the best organization possible. It is not about putting in an honest day's work, but rather, denying reality and the willingness to put forth your best product or service.

The only way you will win is if you stop being complacent and start being focused on discovering ways to simplify production, transform manual activities into automated processes, and update archaic policies that no longer serve the organization well. These actions will result in you cutting costs, streamlining operations, and minimizing idle (and unnecessary) behavior. Maintaining "business as usual" will not generate success, but rather, push you away from being relevant.

This is lost on many. Most organizations try to improve their products and services, but fail to take a truly objective analysis of internal operations. This is unacceptable. You must update and automate. If you do not, you will be wasting time, energy, and resources.

A prime example of this involves a small healthcare company that had steady growth over the course of 10 years yet never adapted to meet the demands of their expanding workforce. One issue involved the extraordinary amount of emails everyone in the company sent and received, and the fatigue that it created. This wasn't always a problem, but as the company grew, hundreds of hours were being wasted each month by employees checking emails that had no relevance to them.

This was particularly noticeable with one process the company put in place when it started 10 years earlier. The company, which consisted of 12 employees at the time, created an email distribution list in which everyone in the company received an email when something related to a patient's medication went wrong. With few patients under their care, this practice served a valuable purpose because it got everyone's attention immediately, allowing them to resolve the issue properly.

The process was effective when the company was small, but as business grew, the policy was never adjusted. This caused a seemingly endless amount of wasted time. At its peak, 200 employees were part of the email group. With as many as 25 patient issues materializing per day, and each issue typically requiring 4 emails to resolve, as many as 20,000 unnecessary emails were being sent and received every day.

After analyzing the situation, a new course of action was put into place. To minimize the unnecessary communication, any employee that discovered an issue with a patient's medication would place the patient's account in a specific queue in the computer program the company used. Based on what type of issue it was, the manager who was monitoring the queue would assign it to a particular employee or team. This simple solution cut hundreds of unproductive hours being wasted by employees reading emails.

When you remain stagnant, refuse to analyze policies, or resist automating processes, you are not operating at the level you should be. Manual labor that could be done with automation, unwillingness to update current processes, and the inability to accept that changes need to be made to improve the business display resistance to optimizing productivity. If you maintain this approach, your company will die.

Stop resisting progress. You need to evolve. Identify how you can update and automate, then make changes to improve your operation.

STOP CELEBRATING MEDIOCRITY, START ELEVATING PERFORMANCE

At the start of 2018, a middle-aged man named Steve joined a weight loss competition hosted by his company. As a significantly obese man, Steve knew he needed to get healthy and believed that joining the competition would instill motivation. In total, over 100 participants from 4 departments joined the 12-week contest to lose weight and get in better shape.

To encourage participants, weekly weigh-ins took place, with the individual who lost the most weight during that week receiving a prize. The contest was set up so that the cumulative total weight lost by participants was not important. Individuals were judged solely on how much weight they lost during that week. The leaders of the contest stated that the contest was set up like that so people wouldn't become discouraged if they weren't doing well.

This flawed concept became evident when Steve was awarded the prize for losing the most weight during the fifth week of the competition. During that week, Steve lost 6 pounds. This could have been seen as a great week for Steve, but he was actually 1 pound heavier than when the contest started. In spite of this, he was still awarded the prize.

This hollow victory meant nothing to Steve. The following week, he put 4 pounds back on. Fast-forwarding to the end, Steve gained 5 pounds during the 12-week competition. He never came close to reaching his goal of being 20 pounds lighter than when the contest started.

Rather than focusing on celebrating exceptional results, the leaders of the competition gave out prizes to people even when their results were subpar. This resulted in 75% of contestants either gaining weight or staying the same.

Six months later, due to a health scare, Steve was once again interested in losing weight. This time it was different. His health had deteriorated so much his very well-being was at stake. No hollow victories would do for this go around. The very essence of his ability to live a normal life was the prize. Not surprisingly, results were much different. In one year, Steve lost over 100 pounds.

The interest in achieving exceptional results only occurs when there is something worth chasing after. Lowering the bar does not instill more motivation, it pushes people toward apathy. There is clearly a difference between losing weight and achieving superior business results, but the core concept remains intact. People are motivated to produce results when they are challenged to work hard and there are legitimate rewards at stake.

Stop building around fake successes and irrelevant metrics. Pandering to the lowest common denominator instills a sense of complacency.

Participation trophies that are undeserved reduce the value of true success. Enabling people to coast through the day causes reduction in productivity.

To be successful, you must hold people to standards that elevate performance. Every time mediocrity is celebrated, it pushes people away from reaching their full potential. Conversely, holding a high standard of excellence forces people to not only put forth considerable effort but also requires them to deliver results. Individuals can no longer revel in comfort and complacency and expect to be rewarded. Instead, they must generate value.

STOP BEING UNPREDICTABLE, START DELIVERING CONSISTENCY

There is a reason why Starbucks flourishes at every location, Harvard only selects the best of the best, and you never see a BMW broken down on the side of the road. These organizations deliver reliable solutions, and this ensures they are able to thrive.

Consistency allows productivity to be measured, creates accountability, establishes and defines reputation, and ensures your message will be clear. Consistency ensures integrity is upheld, enables you to capitalize on opportunities, and helps you push through adversity to reach the finish line. And consistency builds a sturdy foundation that is capable of overcoming adversity and recovering from setbacks. Simply put, consistency enables you to win.[2]

Conversely, being erratic involves having no definitive course of action and creates uncertainty. Being erratic eliminates the ability to build long-term success while causing people to put up physical, emotional, and virtual barriers. And being erratic causes uneasiness, provokes confusion, and reduces trust. Simply put, being erratic destroys relevance.

When looking at these two options, there is no question in which direction you should go. The advanced competition that is present in every industry and market make consistency essential and erraticism a direct path to insignificance.

The truth is, every stakeholder in your company wants to have their expectations met with minimal surprises, regardless of the situation. Steady communication, reliable experiences, and a dependable approach toward delivering value create a sense of tranquility. And with competition being as intense as it is, the opportunity for organizations to deviate from where they excel and be callous with how they operate their business while remaining successful is fleeting.

Organizations must instead be hyper-focused on their core competency and double down on delivering products and services that align with their competitive advantage. The need to change to adapt to consumer demand is necessary, but completely abandoning what has made you successful will cause your consumers to look for other options and your enterprise to fold. Starbucks, Harvard, and BMW understand this. They know they must maintain a consistent operation to be successful, and that is exactly why people look at them with such esteem. To experience the same outcome, you must establish a similar approach. You must deliver consistency.

However, while consistency is key, it cannot be an excuse for you not to change or find ways to improve. For example, Starbucks' competitive advantage involves providing customers high-quality coffee in high-traffic areas. They do not allow themselves to rest here. They are always upgrading the way they treat their customers. Most recently, they created an app in which their guests can order their drink and pay prior to arriving at the store. This allows the customer to walk into Starbucks and pick up their beverage, without waiting in line. Starbucks hasn't strayed away from their expertise or what they do best, they just added to it.

You must employ the same approach. Delivering consistency must align with change that will make your organization better and improve the customer experience. This will increase the value you deliver.

STOP ACCEPTING COMPLACENCY, START BEING PROACTIVE

While consistency is essential, complacency is catastrophic. Those who are complacent lose. Rather than storming ahead working to achieve greatness, complacent companies push forward just enough to be content, for the interim, until something disrupts their happiness bubble.

This is a terrible way to run a business. It creates a constant state of waiting for things to change or fall apart prior to putting forth effort to improve. In essence, you are at the mercy of external forces, instead of being in control of your own destiny. When thinking about it from this perspective, it is unattractive. No one wants their external environment to be the sole driving force of everything they do.

Bringing this down to a personal level, this is why people work hard to sacrifice short-term happiness for long-term fulfillment and do what is necessary to improve their life and the lives of those around them. Their desire for success trumps their willingness to accept where they are currently. This is the difference between people who are looking to just cover the bills versus people who are interested in building long-lasting financial freedom. Those willing to look beyond the short term and make sacrifices for the future have considerably more opportunities.

The same is the case for businesses. The willingness to put forth extra effort and refusal to remain comfortable consistently wins. Yet, too many times, companies find a process, an application, a product, or a service they like and refuse to move away from it due to the success it initially brought. Rather than looking for ways to improve, the business goes on cruise control as complacency and comfort set in. This level of contentment remains until their external environment changes and a new approach is needed.

Companies that have instilled this methodology have always struggled, but it has become even more problematic in recent years. For example, the hapless effort of Payless Shoes to establish a quality online presence, AOLs inept attempts at moving from dial-up internet to Wi-Fi, and Yahoo!'s inability to successfully change from a portal to more progressive web services all highlight an unwillingness to change if not prompted. Each ended with catastrophic results.

If you wait for the world to tell you to change, you have already lost. Business simply moves too fast for you to wait. If you truly want to stay viable, you must be comfortable being uncomfortable and you must continually look for ways to improve. The products and services you created yesterday will not meet the demands of your customers tomorrow. There is nothing you can do about external forces and the way the market evolves, so you need to be obsessed with what you can control. This ownership enables you to modify your internal scope to meet the external environment you encounter head-on.

This may seem excessive, but if you do not choose to push forward, someone else will, and they will ultimately push you out. The level of competition in every industry, market, and environment creates the need for businesses to constantly transform the way they operate in every capacity, and it will not stop.

If you accept complacency over being proactive, you will die. Complacency is the enemy of success and will ultimately chip away at any competitive advantage you ever had. Stop being complacent. To win, you must be proactive.

BRINGING IT ALL TOGETHER

These seven areas of focus are not the only actions companies must emphasize, but they will provide you a better opportunity to maximize the value you deliver. The truth is, there is very little margin for error in the workplace in this day and age. The implications from every decision made are magnified due to the competitiveness within every industry and market. This means you must continually adapt and evolve to optimize results. By embracing these seven areas of focus, business operations can be streamlined, and employees will be encouraged to put forth optimal effort, ultimately generating a stronger, more agile organization that is capable of producing exceptional results.

NOTES

1. Prisco, Jacopo. "Why UPS Trucks (Almost) Never Turn Left." *CNN.com.* www.cnn.com/2017/02/16/world/ups-trucks-no-left-turns/index.html (accessed April 10, 2020).
2. Holtzclaw, Eric. "Power of Consistency: 5 Rules." *Inc.com.* www.inc.com/eric-v-holtzclaw/consistency-power-success-rules.html (accessed April 10, 2020).

Section IV

What's Next?

Globalization, technological advances, and changes in the way people live and work have created a new recipe for success in business and has generated a tidal wave of disruption in every industry and market in the world. Take heed in this extraordinary transformation and treat it as a warning. Businesses that had loyal customers have already closed their doors permanently because of an inability to meet the new demands of the market. If you do not change, you will be next.

There is no greater risk to your business in today's environment than attempting to remain the same. While you may make excuses as to why you do not need to change and justify reasons to avoid adapting, the end of your road is predictable if you do not transform. You will die.

The only way to succeed is to embrace the four core questions. Connect these questions to how it relates to your industry, market, and business. Determine what value you currently deliver to consumers and how you will need to change to continue delivering value by objectively answering these questions:

- What do you do?
- What could make you obsolete or replaceable?

- What change can you make to eliminate this risk?
- What specific actions can you take to execute this change?

What could not be foreseen in business in the past is now reality, and how you handle the changes that are taking place in your industry and market today will inevitably mold what your business looks like in the future. The unimaginable is here. The need to level up is present. And the time for action is now. Because the truth is, unless you build a foundation that is grounded in the extraordinary transformations that are occurring now, and will continue to occur in the future, you will not last.

10

The Unimaginable

Have you ever thought about putting your nicest clothes on and driving down to the coast and into the harbor so you can wave goodbye to a ship that is heading out to sea?

Of course not.

If anyone suggested this idea, they would be laughed at and ridiculed. Yet numerous decades ago, people flocked to the shoreline in their finest attire to wave at a boat until it disappeared over the horizon. And almost no one who participated in this activity knew a single passenger on the ship.

Many years from now, people will be equally shocked about the things that we choose to spend our time on. For example, millions of adults watch a television show about a recently married couple looking to buy their first home, and children all over the world spend countless hours watching other kids (they don't know) play video games online. Truth be told, waving at a boat, watching other people buy a house on TV, and observing kids play video games on the internet are all odd behaviors. Yet for some reason, in certain circles at different points in time, these actions are viewed as normal.

The overarching concept is the same: technology, social movements, and access to information affect the way people live their lives and inevitably cause the world to change. This disrupts the way industries function, markets shift, and businesses operate. What was unimaginable a few years ago is now the norm, and what is seen as incomprehensible today will be commonplace in the future.

It is essential to get ahead of this by eliminating the notion that what you are doing currently will work in the years to come. Every industry, market, and environment will continue to go through extraordinary transformations, requiring every company to change as well. And while this has always been the case, changes in the world are happening faster than ever, causing markets to fluctuate with increased frequency and variance.

To be fair, change in business has always been present. However, what is different is that changes now occur in the blink of an eye, often without notice. This means you must be comfortable being uncomfortable. Resisting the urge to change and reminiscing about how things were better in years past will not have a positive effect on the outcome of the future. It will only push you away from being relevant.

The world has changed, and the unimaginable has now invaded every part of the business ecosystem. This will not stop. Instead, the unimaginable will continue to affect industries and markets throughout the world, requiring you to transform your operation.

THE UNIMAGINABLE MADE YOUR COMPETITIVE ADVANTAGE OBSOLETE

At one point in time, Best Buy was the ultimate electronics store. Walking into any Best Buy location brought a sense of energy and excitement that shoppers wouldn't soon forget. Every store featured a huge showroom with every type of technology you could possibly want. From TVs and DVD players to computers and home appliances, access to every kind of device, machine, game, and toy made Best Buy the place to shop for the most amazing products and services.

At the height of its success in the early 2000s, Best Buy had over 1,100 stores located in all 50 states, Washington D.C., and Puerto Rico. This made their competitive advantage quite simple. They were everywhere and had every type of electronic device you could possibly want, enabling customers to pick up a product or purchase a service quickly and easily.[1]

However, while Best Buy was doing well, new, online competitors began to emerge. This caused many of Best Buy's traditional competition to go out of business. There were many reasons for this, but a primary sticking point was the ability for online retailers to sell at lower prices than brick and mortar stores due to lower fixed costs. Traditional storefronts and retail employees were expenses online vendors didn't have to worry about.

To add to this challenge was the way many shoppers purchased their goods. In many cases, customers would walk through stores, try various types of products and services, then settle on the exact make and model they wanted. However, rather than having the cashier ring up their merchandise, the prospective shopper would write down the model number and then go online to purchase at a lower price.

This caused Best Buy's competitive advantage to turn into a detriment. Carrying every type of product and service and having stores strategically placed in high traffic areas allowed people to pop in and test equipment, only to go home and purchase online.

Many companies have run into problems similar to this. Resting on the laurels of past successes due to a competitive advantage that is no longer relevant causes companies to die. This is particularly hard to understand today because of the way technological advances have shifted the landscape of the business world so quickly. Robotics minimize labor costs in factories, websites make purchasing products and services simpler, quicker, and less expensive than going into stores, and electronic self-checkout eliminates the need for human involvement with common activities like paying for items at the grocery store.

So, while your competitive advantage likely created distance from competitors initially, technological innovations, streamlined service, and changes in social norms eliminate these advantages. This requires you to rethink the way you approach your business. If you have not adjusted your sails on how to meet the new demands of the market, you are already behind. Your dynamite competitive advantage due to business connections, premier merchandise, financial capital, barriers to entry, or the location of your stores has vanished because of external drivers that have come into play.

The unimaginable has made your competitive advantage obsolete. You must recalibrate and determine how you will move forward so you can capitalize on the new way your industry or market functions.

THE UNIMAGINABLE CHANGED THE GAME

Transformational change has always occurred and will always occur in the world.

In 2010, if someone would have told you that you would be comfortable getting into a complete stranger's car, so that the stranger would take you somewhere you wanted to go, you never would have believed it. In 2016, there were 45 million monthly users of Uber.[2]

In 2013, if someone would have told you that millions of people would order groceries online and have it delivered to their door, you would have rolled your eyes. In 2018, there were $23.9 billion of digital grocery sales in the United States. That number is expected to increase to almost $60 billion by 2023.[3]

In 2016, if someone would have told you that the next social media craze would be 15-second music and dance videos, you never would have listened to them. In April of 2020, the TikTok app had been downloaded more than 2 billion times.[4]

Though all of these changes were inconceivable just a few years before they actually happened, they are now seen as commonplace. Stretch to think about what could happen to *your* industry, market, or business that is unimaginable currently.

Because of the digital takeover, every company is at risk. Yet, in spite of how much the business world has changed and the advances in technology have affected every part of our lives, companies remain fixated on using outdated and irrelevant strategies and place prominence on products and services that fail to generate the returns they desire.

You cannot maintain the same operation and expect to be successful. Your business does not operate in a vacuum. The rules are different. While you might not like it and it might not give you the advantage you had previously, you cannot expect to win by playing the game with rules that are no longer applicable.

This is equally important for multinational corporations and small businesses. The way you used to operate is now irrelevant. So, whether you were the big bully on the block that everyone needed to cater to or the small mom and pop shop that was the only game in town, life is no longer the same. The unimaginable changed the game. This requires you to change the way your business functions.

THE UNIMAGINABLE IS EVERYWHERE

When people go to an appointment at a doctor's office, they typically follow a fairly uniform process. They take time off work, drive to their appointment, check in at the front desk, and sit in the lobby waiting for their name to be called while scrolling through their phone. After finally being summoned by the Medical Assistant, they are escorted to the exam room, where the Medical Assistant verifies personal information and checks their vitals before the nurse comes in to discuss any health concerns they are currently experiencing. After all of that, the doctor comes in to complete the examination. The process is long and cumbersome, yet is accepted because there has never been a better alternative.

This is changing. Many physicians are now bringing care to their patients through telemedicine instead of expecting them to physically go to their office. With video chat services just a click away, physicians are now treating their patients virtually. Understandably, all medical treatments cannot be performed through telemedicine, but certain measures can be done with the use of technology that eliminates excessive wastes of time traditional processes take.

There may be no industry that is more heavily regulated than the medical field, with privacy and safety emphasized above all else. Yet, even within this industry, the tide has started to turn. Though the idea of having an appointment online to address medical issues was beyond anything most could fathom 10 years ago, Doctor's offices are now adopting this practice with greater regularity than ever before.

Altering business practices to shorten inconveniences, minimize disruptions, and streamline life is happening everywhere. From adopting telemedicine and having groceries delivered to our homes to using Uber and Lyft to take us places and downloading bank apps so we can cash checks instantly, the practice of eliminating unnecessary wastes of time to simplify daily life is now a regular occurrence. And while you may believe your company is immune to these changes and your industry is safe from the technological advances that are occurring throughout the world, if you take inventory of your surroundings, it will be clear that you are wrong.

The unimaginable is stretching across every industry, market, and environment in the world, and if you are not willing to jump on board, you will be left behind. The desire to optimize every part of life is in every one of us, so the idea that you can avoid streamlining an area within your business to enhance the customer experience is false.

The unimaginable is everywhere. This requires you to discover ways to improve your operation at any cost.

THE UNIMAGINABLE HAPPENED

For those who believe that the unimaginable won't happen, you don't need to look back too far to know that everything can change in an instant. As referenced earlier, in 2020, COVID-19 flipped every industry and market upside down and caused the entire world to push pause while chaos and uncertainty filled communities everywhere.

Prior to COVID-19, no one could have predicted that anyone who went out in public would need to wear a protective mask and gloves and use "social distancing" as a way to remain safe and healthy, or that the vast majority of people who were employed would either be working from home, laid off, or furloughed. Yet this was the case.

COVID-19 caused every part of life to change. Businesses in every industry shut down, children across the world stopped going to school, and sporting events, weddings, birthdays, and church services were canceled. Additionally, families were fragmented, with loved ones being forced to communicate with relatives through online video chats rather than in person. And if there was a possibility that you had the virus, you were forced to self-quarantine for 14 days.

Many businesses never recovered. For those that did, their operation was never the same. COVID-19 left an indelible mark on every industry and market in the world; changes in online buying, delivery services, work from home, travel, and virtual communication all stemmed from the pandemic.

The notion that the unimaginable cannot happen again is wrong. The potential for exceptional transformation to occur in the blink of an eye is always a threat. Though the probability of another transformational change flipping every industry and market upside down in an instant is unlikely in the near future, the unimaginable will happen again soon. It will just be on a smaller scale and look different.

It could be your biggest competitor coming out with a product that completely changes your industry, your best customer shutting down their plant located 2 miles from your company, or new policies and regulations requiring you to transform how you do business.

This type of scenario happens all the time, and companies aren't ready for it. Nor are they asking the right questions.

Can you keep your production facility and change your product? Keep your product and change your customer? Keep your customer and modify your delivery? Grow your customer base and change your delivery? Or take advantage of the new situation to scale up and partner with a new business? Or maybe it is something completely different.

Regardless of the action you take, the rationale that the unimaginable is impossible is false. The unimaginable happened and will happen again. This requires you to think outside the box and identify what course of action you will take and how you will generate value when it does.

THE UNIMAGINABLE REQUIRES YOU TO TAKE ACTION

On November 12, 2019, The Walt Disney Company launched their latest service, *Disney+*, a subscription video-on-demand streaming platform. The service primarily distributes films and television series produced by Walt Disney Studios and Walt Disney Television and features content from Marvel, National Geographic, Pixar, and Star Wars. Prior to launching this platform, Disney used streaming services from other companies to share its product. Though this was working fine, it did not maximize Disney's bottom line, nor did it enable the company to maintain complete control of its content.

Disney, one of the most recognized and celebrated brands in the world, didn't have to launch this new service. It was already a 5-Star organization that delivered premium value to its customer base with magical theme parks, captivating movies, and unique merchandise. Yet they refuse to be content, and that is exactly why they are one of the most successful companies in the world.

If you want to have sustained success as well, you must adopt a similar approach. You must constantly adapt and evolve, while placing emphasis on developing new products and services that consumers demand. You must also remove outdated merchandise, archaic technology, and business models that lack relevance and sniff out practices, processes, and people that are not geared toward building for the future, and you must do it now.

Waiting for the perfect time instead of taking action lacks rationale. People will try to convince you otherwise, but there truly is no ideal time to make changes. Failing to make a move because you believe you aren't vulnerable is unreasonable, and waiting to see if your business model becomes relevant again lacks logic.

This may seem too simplistic in nature, but it carries merit in every aspect of business. Too many companies have built a comfort-centered approach instead of identifying ways to optimize their operation. This causes them to become vulnerable and ultimately lose their competitive advantage. This is what happened to companies like A&P, Gander Mountain, and Sports Authority. They all accepted that their business models could withstand the unimaginable changes that were occurring in their external environment, while putting the glory from years past on a pedestal. And they all suffered because of it.

Retail companies are a prime example, but they are not the only industry that is at risk. Every business in every industry must place emphasis on taking action. Even technology-based firms that live in an exclusively virtual space can be overtaken without notice. For example, Classmates.com, Friendster, and Myspace all had a shot at being the company that would change the world with social media, yet failed because they did not place emphasis on what the customers wanted or where the market was going. They all had a set agenda on what they wanted to do and wouldn't pivot regardless of what the market was telling them. This resulted in users moving away from these platforms and toward sites like Facebook, Twitter, Instagram, and Snapchat.

These examples highlight what can take place if you do not transition your business to meet the new demands of the market. The market's allegiance to a particular brand, label, or product line is nonexistent. This puts the onus on you to continually invest time and effort into improving products, optimizing services, and cutting costs. While it is not always pleasant to be agile and adjust to the constant changes the market goes through, you must take this challenge on if you want to remain in business long term.

This has never been more important than it is today. The world is moving faster than ever, so the opportunity to delay decision-making is gone. In order to win in your industry, you must produce results as quickly and efficiently as possible. Stop denying reality. Stop listening to those around you who say that you don't need to change. And stop talking yourself out of taking decisive action, especially when the unimaginable takes place.

You must determine what you want to do and where you want to go and move in that direction. There is no way around it. The unimaginable requires you to take action.

BRINGING IT ALL TOGETHER

People now rent baby clothes online rather than buy them in a store, receive packages delivered by drones instead of getting them through traditional delivery carriers, and control every electronic device in their home with their smartphone in place of operating manually. These services were all unimaginable just a few years ago.

The unimaginable has invaded every industry and market, and if you do not make changes to your business, the unimaginable will result in you no longer being in business. Everything you have done up to this point will not enable you to win in the future. You must objectively assess your business and the way your industry is transforming and then take action by adapting, evolving, and improving. The unimaginable is the new normal, and if you do not get on board, you will die.

NOTES

1. Statista.com. "Total Number of Best Buy Stores in the United States from 2008 to 2020, by Segment." *Statista.com*. www.statista.com/statistics/249558/total-numb er-of-best-buy-stores-in-the-united-states-by-segment/ (accessed April 12, 2020).
2. Smith, Craig. "110 Amazing Uber Statistics, Demographics and Facts (2020)." *ExpandedRamblings.com*. https://expandedramblings.com/index.php/uber-stati stics/ (accessed May 23, 2020).
3. Ross, Lisa. "US Online Grocery Shopping – Statistics and Trends (Infographic)." *Invespcro.com*. www.invespcro.com/blog/us-online-grocery-shopping/ (accessed May 23, 2020).
4. Chapple, Craig. "TikTok Crosses 2 Billion Downloads After Best Quarter For Any App Ever." SensorTower.com. https://sensortower.com/blog/tiktok-downloads-2-bi llion (accessed August 27,2020).

11

Level Up

In 2013, DreamWorks Animation created *The Croods*, a movie about a prehistoric family whose lives are in peril after a massive earthquake destroys their home. Much to the dismay of the patriarchal father who is fearful of change, the family journeys across a dangerous land in search of a new residence.

While traversing through the unknown, they develop a relationship with an innovative prodigy who has unique ways of assessing problems and discovering solutions. This causes a rift in the family with a struggle for supremacy materializing as the overbearing father's archaic way of thinking is continually passed over for the resourceful young man's innovative ideas. However, after the family dodges numerous close calls due to the father's unwillingness to evolve, he finally sees how the phenom's method of survival is better. This causes him to change his approach and work with the young man to save his family and find a new place to live.[1]

This is obviously an extreme example from an animated movie, but it hits home in many ways. Change can be difficult for people, especially those who have been following a certain course of action for a long time. The same is true for organizations. The world has changed and the need to adapt has never been stronger, but some businesses instinctively resist. They push forward with behavior that is in direct contrast to the changes that have occurred in the business world for interest in maintaining the same approach they have always had.

If this is you, abandon this mentality immediately!

The importance of adapting to meet the new demands of the market is paramount. Yet for some reason, in spite of all that has happened and all that has transformed, there is still an inherent interest in fighting change. Maintaining consistency and keeping the status quo will not cut it. You must accept that you need to level up to be successful. Below are five actions you must take to level up.

START BELIEVING THE TRUTH

Whether we are willing to accept it or not, in order to consistently win, you must change. This is not appealing for many companies (and people). Having worked hard to develop valuable products and services and acquire coveted customers, the idea of making change is unattractive. So, instead of accepting the inevitable need to adapt, many businesses react to changes in the workplace by pushing back. The status quo is so much easier than actively pursuing an alternative way to operate.

This is often because there is a level of mystery that comes along with every change, and this unknown causes people to have a sense of discomfort that they would like to avoid. This causes many people to deny reality and revert back to what is comfortable, instead of taking a risk and making a change.

If you choose not to evolve in business, you are choosing to die. While businesses can typically withstand changes for the short term, continual interest in fighting change causes companies to not only miss out on opportunities for growth but quite often eliminates the ability for them to maintain relevance at all. This is especially true in today's climate. With increased technology, specialization at every part of the value chain, and extraordinary shifts in the landscape of business taking place faster than ever, change is not an option, it is a necessity.

Nevertheless, there are still companies, leaders, and employees who view change as a choice rather than a requirement. This type of thinking is off base and will lead you to dismal results. Nothing ever remains the same. The world, and all that is in it, is constantly changing.

To level up, you must start believing the truth. There is no other choice and no other way to compete.

STOP TRYING TO BE RIGHT, WORRY ABOUT *GETTING* IT RIGHT!

So many people (and organizations) are focused on being right, rather than getting it right. Instead of pivoting the business to deliver more profitable returns, finding a solution that will create optimal results, or being open to possibilities that extend beyond the finite approach that was successful in the past, many people (and organizations) remain shortsighted and self-focused. They want to maintain the status quo over transforming into something better, are committed to winning the argument instead of looking for new ways to develop, and resist empowering others so they can promote their own agenda. Their obsession for being right trumps all else.

The truth is for many people (and organizations), being right is the essence of validating their worth, showcasing their intelligence, and proving that their decision-making is superior. Instead of implementing the best course of action, they push their own agenda, even if it is a detriment to the organization as a whole. This enables them to feel important and justify their status. This could involve an unwillingness to leverage technology to be more efficient, use social media to create a digital footprint, or admit that a certain business decision, product line, or innovation is no longer competitive.

These people (and organizations) have a particular point of view, ideology, or perspective, and regardless of what is learned, will not change their position. Instead, to back up their point of view, they surround themselves with likeminded individuals, find websites that validate their beliefs, and read articles from years past that promote the ideologies they are unwilling to move on from. They are not looking for information. They want affirmation.

If your path fails to align with what the market is telling you, you are resistant to the changes that others in your industry are making, or your products and services are no longer jumping off the shelves, you must recalibrate. While it is much easier to highlight the outliers who have made large fortunes by blazing their own trail than swallowing your pride and admitting you are wrong, it is unwise to bet on the exception over the rule.

The work environment is moving too fast and changing too rapidly to maintain an outdated approach toward business. Instead, you must take inventory of your surroundings and adapt as you go. Failure is informative and can lead to the discovery of the proper solution. Conversely, maintaining your perspective regardless of facts and data is narrow-mindedness and a recipe for disaster.

To level up, you must stop trying to be right and worry about getting it right. Changing your direction based on the way the market shifts is the only way to be successful.

START AUDITING YOUR SURROUNDINGS

Certain people inevitably remain around you for extended periods of time. Your roommate from college whom you have a deep affinity for, the Director of the Marketing Department who has been in the organization for years, and the mentor you've always looked up to all have a special place in your heart.

While these individuals have rooted themselves in your world, it is important to acknowledge the changes that have occurred in your environment since your initial connection with them. Your college roommate was always fun to be around, but what do you really have in common with him now? Do you share the same values, goals, and priorities 25 years later? Or is he just there because you are accustomed to him? The Director of Marketing was pivotal when the company launched 2 decades ago, but she hasn't adapted her mentality at all over that time. What value does she generate for the company today? And the mentor you always looked up to was a huge success in business, but he has been retired for 15 years and doesn't know anything about the digital age. What is he really doing for your business?

Looking in the rearview mirror, these people seem like they are still valuable commodities to your business. However, when you look at what is ahead, the picture could look quite different. The value they deliver to your business today is most likely nominal.

To be successful, you must audit your surroundings.

Businesses throughout the world are relying on people who haven't produced in years, instead of objectively analyzing performance and assessing what the future will look like. Past successes are nice to reflect on, but they do not always properly indicate what is to come. As heartless as it may sound, to be successful, you must audit your surroundings. If there are people who fail to produce any tangible results and lack foundational value that is required to succeed in this new business environment, they need to go. This is difficult for some. The willingness to let go is challenging. Steadiness is a valued attribute, and making a transformational shift can be undesirable. And this is exactly why organizations fail.

Ideas and words do not generate success, it is actions and execution. Yet time and again, the words expressed about change and being proactive end up being merely lip service for the masses. This is unacceptable.

Long-standing employees, legacy programs, and ingrained processes can all be extremely valuable, but they also have the potential to stop you from optimizing performance. To be successful, you need to make difficult decisions by analyzing your internal and external environment and assessing what is holding you back and what can enable you to improve.

To level up, you must start auditing your surroundings.

STOP BEING COMFORT-CENTERED

Success in almost any industry is predicated on numerous workings that include determination, calculated decisions, hard work, and precise timing. But success also comprises the willingness to voice concerns, ask questions when something doesn't make sense, and stand up for what you know to be true. Not surprisingly, the willingness to share reservations about your company or what could be improved is not always appealing. So, instead of rocking the boat, people just coast along while passively patronizing everything the company does, often times, without analyzing the situation or identifying if it is the right decision.

This is a recipe for disaster.

Companies that have a culture in which everyone puts one foot in front of the other while failing to look up to see if they are headed toward success or off the edge of a cliff will inevitably fail. Validating every action and blindly following orders epitomizes a lack of critical thinking and instills a false sense of confidence that will not produce the positive results the company is interested in achieving.

Building a cohesive unit is important; however, maintaining harmony in place of discovering the best path is not the answer. The necessity of having at least some level of friction is required for a business to be successful. In order to grow, you must push against blind acceptance and the willingness to conform.

Yet no one wants to do this, especially when you are succeeding as an organization. Making considerable transformations when all is well is unpopular. However, the success you have is not sustainable if you do not continue to adapt and evolve.

Your contentment will ultimately drive your business away from reaching its full potential. Reject the urge to accept life as you have always known it and push back against patronizing everything your company does. Success in the present day is only valuable if you are able to build on it for the future. There are organizations in the world today that are focused on capitalizing on the gaps in your system so that they can put you out of business.

If you do not change, you will be opening the door for them to succeed and you will blend in with every other organization until you eventually become irrelevant. Impractical visions for how the market will remain steady to meet your outdated ideals do you no good. Push back against being comfort-centered and fight against the urge to justify every decision your company makes.

Changes in the business world are coming faster, are more intense, and have greater consequences than ever before. This means you need to stop being content. Determine what you want to do and where you want to go. This will ultimately enable you to build for the future.

To level up, you must stop being comfort-centered.

START TRULY COMMITTING

In the early 1990s, Joe Rohde, a Walt Disney Imagineer, was fascinated by the idea of bringing a "living" theme park to Disneyworld. He wasn't alone in this dream. The company had always wanted to use live animals in the parks but was never able to find a way.

Rohde believed he could make it happen, and he had a plan to do it. Rohde pitched his idea to Disney's senior leadership team. He shared a detailed layout for a new park that included a 100-acre safari, movie theaters, concessions scattered throughout the park, and an enormous parking lot.

He was promptly rejected. He was told Disney wasn't interested in having a zoo.

Though disappointed, Rohde went back to the drawing board and came back a second time with a similar pitch. This time he upped his game; he brought charts, graphs, and data to explain why his idea would create an unbelievable atmosphere and how it was a perfect fit for Disney. Once again, he was told no.

Most people would have given up then, but Rohde decided to give it one last try. After analyzing what went wrong with his first two attempts, he decided to change his strategy. He needed to bring his pitch to life, and he knew exactly how to do it.

Halfway through his third time explaining his idea, a fully grown Siberian Tiger walked into the room. Everyone froze at the sight of the magnificent beast, with leadership suddenly understanding the power, magnitude, and sheer magic that enchanting and exotic animals from across the world could bring to the Disney experience. Not long after, Rohde was given the green light to start building what would later be known as Disney's Animal Kingdom.[2]

It is not necessary (or advised) to bring in a Siberian Tiger to make your point, but you do need to go all in. When engaging in transformational change, merely going through the motions is not enough. You must truly commit.

Apathetic attempts at leveling up are similar to people who post on Facebook they need a new job yet fail to put forth an honest effort applying for roles or connecting with recruiters, individuals who state they are tired of being single though never step out of their comfort zone to meet new people, and friends who share they are interested in getting in shape but don't eat right and never exercise. Words and half-hearted efforts get you nowhere.

If you want a better job, you need to search for new opportunities and network. If you want to be in a relationship, you must find suitable mates who are single. And if you are interested in getting in shape, you need to eat right and hit the gym. Half-assed approaches toward achieving a goal and ill-advised attempts at execution will only bring you disappointment.

This is true in business as well. Going halfway won't cut it. You need to truly commit to win. The days of companies being fat and happy and coasting to easy victories are over. In today's business environment, everyone wants a bigger piece of the pie. And with the mode of entry now easier than ever in almost every industry and market in the world, it makes it that much more competitive.

This challenge has become even more of an issue recently due to companies developing "shiny object syndrome." At its very core, shiny object syndrome is an ailment that stymies companies (and people) that are always chasing after the latest and greatest thing. Much like how a child will play with a shiny new toy for a short period of time only to cast it off for something newer and shinier, so too are companies at risk of chasing after the latest and greatest concept, product, or service for the interim, only to change direction and go after something different without seeing the first idea to the finish line.

It is undeniable companies must adapt and evolve to be successful, but obsessively changing directions numerous times will cause organizations to implode. Bouncing from idea to idea, or switching to the latest tools, techniques, products, or services simply because something new is on the market, is a recipe for disaster. It will reduce productivity and destroy morale.

If you don't go all in, you won't succeed. Weak attempts and apathetic efforts won't cut it. Neither will chasing after the latest gadget, tool, product, or service.

To level up, you must truly commit.

BRINGING IT ALL TOGETHER

If you are stranded out in the desert, you don't start searching for a source to drink from after you become dehydrated; you begin searching immediately. This aligns closely with the way you should approach change in your business. Your interest in improving your company and leveling up shouldn't begin when you are starting to fade, but rather, be an ongoing area of focus.

This is evident from the demise of all the companies that believed they didn't need to improve operations, upgrade technology platforms, and change outdated business models because they were already reaping the benefits of hard work. Regardless of the industry you are in, market you are trying to capture, or business you are leading, the necessity of leveling up is real. Companies that fail to make a concerted effort, choosing instead to maintain the status quo, will not survive. The speed at which business is moving and change is occurring will not allow it to survive. So, unless you are building for the future and finding ways to improve your operation today, you will not make it.

You must level up.

NOTES

1. Sanders, Chris and Kirk DeMicco. *The Croods*. DVD. Directed by Chris Sanders and Kirk DeMicco. Universal City, CA: Universal Pictures Home Entertainment, 2013.
2. Bell, Brittney. "The Tiger in the Room: How Joe Rohde Pitched Animal Kingdom." *Dizavenue.com*. www.dizavenue.com/2017/02/the-tiger-in-room-how-joe-roh de-pitched.html?m=1 (accessed April 12, 2020).

12

Ten Changes That Will Transform the Business World over the Next 10 Years

There are many areas organizations will need to invest in to compete in the future and many ways companies will need to transform to be successful. However, these changes are often hidden by misguided beliefs, inaccurate assessments, and irrational ideals.

The future of business is complex, intricate, and matrixed. It focuses on leveraging synergies and capitalizing on efficiencies and involves creativity and transparency. It is undeniable that changes will take place over the course of the next decade, but the path ahead is not clear. However, there are certain inevitabilities that cannot be argued. The following are 10 of the many changes that will have an enormous impact on the future of business over the next 10 years:

- Automation and artificial intelligence
- Data analytics
- The Internet of Things
- Apps and mobile devices
- Money management
- Expanded home delivery
- The death of television advertising
- The gig economy
- Reskilling the workforce
- Functionality over formality

Identifying the changes that will take place over the next decade can be beneficial, but it will only create value if you can take advantage of them in your business. It is on you to determine how you will respond to the impending changes that will occur over the next decade. This chapter will go through each of the 10 changes that will take place and provide probing questions to help you leverage these changes to help you generate better outcomes.

1. AUTOMATION AND ARTIFICIAL INTELLIGENCE

Automation is the use of technology by which a process or procedure is performed with limited or no human involvement. Artificial Intelligence (AI) is technology designed to perform tasks commonly associated with human thinking and decision-making. These technological advances are very different. However, in this context they will be connected, knowing that both involve replacing human work with technology and/or robots.

The use of automation and AI is already taking place in almost every industry and market in the world and will continue to increase over the next decade. Due to a never-ending battle to cut costs and streamline service, and automated tools being more reliable and able to run around the clock, the replacement of manual labor with automation will continue to increase dramatically.

This will create a transformational shift in the way businesses operate and employees are used. No longer will companies be able to remain competitive in their industry by relying on employees to perform manual labor that can be completed by machines.

Industries that will transform the most because of automation and AI are:

- *Manufacturing*: Manufacturing has always been at the forefront of automation and AI, making it no surprise that it will continue to lead the charge in the future. Enabling robots to assemble products is faster, simplifies production, and reduces errors.
- *Packaging and shipping*: The delivery of physical items has already been affected by automation and AI and will see considerable impacts in the future. Due to continual advances and the repetitive process that comes with delivering goods, expanding automation and AI in the packaging and shipping industry is a natural fit and will

drastically reduce the time, effort, and financial resources required to deliver goods. Companies are already leveraging systems to simplify the process, with adoption expected to continue as frontrunners like Amazon and Walmart find innovative ways to fulfill orders. Within the next 10 years, companies will package goods and deliver to their final destination, all without any human intervention.

- *Customer service*: Frontline employees who serve as customer service agents will continue to decrease over the course of the next decade as they are replaced by machines. From computers that take your order at McDonald's and self-checkout machines at the grocery store to voice-automated customer service agents taking your phone calls and machines that process orders online, the need for human interaction is becoming less and less. In the future, technology will become so sophisticated that you won't know when you are speaking with a human and when you are communicating with a robot.

- *Financial services*: With an advanced ability to develop highly complex financial models and predict stock trends based on market data, the need for human involvement in the financial industry is declining. In its place are finely tuned systems that deliver expert analysis on financial matters, both big and small. These transformations won't come overnight. However, the vast amount of financial data and significance of making timely decisions will push companies toward increased reliance on leveraging technologically savvy programs.

- *Healthcare*: Hospitals, healthcare companies, and doctors' offices are becoming increasingly reliant on automation and AI for a variety of medical activities and procedures. Areas in which robots particularly excel involve diagnosing diseases, delivering anesthesia, and performing surgery. As technology becomes more sophisticated, their accuracy and dependability will surpass human healthcare providers, making automation and AI no longer an option for healthcare companies but a necessity.

- *Agriculture*: The grueling hours of farming are not likely to disappear anytime soon, but with advanced technological equipment now becoming the norm, manual labor has dropped considerably. This trend will continue with the increased use of drones to survey land, cultivation tools to optimize the amount of produce crops yield, satellites that can measure the moisture in the ground, and simulation modeling applications to determine the best time to harvest.

- *Transportation*: Fully autonomous vehicles will have exponential growth over the next decade. This will initially be with personal vehicles. Self-driving trucks transporting goods will follow. At the end of the decade, autonomous air travel will be available.[1]

Taking Action

The transition away from manual labor and toward automation and AI puts those who resist adoption in peril. Automation and AI are levers for increased efficiency, reduction in costs, and optimized productivity, and if you don't jump on board, you will be on the outside looking in. You must identify where you can change so that you are able to keep up with the competition and maintain a competitive advantage.

- What processes are you completing manually that you could automate?
- What are industry leaders doing that you could adopt?
- What could you invest in to reduce variable costs?

2. DATA ANALYTICS

Data analytics involves analyzing data to make more informed business decisions. This ultimately leads to a better ability to accurately predict what your industry, market, business, and customer will do. The use of data analytics (and big data) has grown considerably since the turn of the millennia and will continue to grow over the next decade. This is primarily because the ability to properly analyze data enables companies to invest their time, talents, and resources in the right places so that they can maximize their return on investment and minimize risk. Areas that will be of particular importance over the next 10 years include:

- *Customer buying habits*: Knowing what people are buying and what they will purchase next is an enormous advantage for companies. By analyzing data properly, businesses are able to detect customer purchasing patterns with better accuracy. This enables them to market the right products and services to the right consumers at the perfect time.
- *Market trend analysis*: Along with monitoring buying habits of individual customers, companies are now better able to track online

activity, point of sale transactions, and dynamic changes in customer trends. This study of human behavior enables businesses to use a more targeted approach for attracting the right customers. By segmenting the market properly, the ability to focus on the appropriate audience can happen every time. This has grown increasingly effective through the use of social media advertising.

- *Risk management*: Risks associated with an organization's workflow are always present. Through proper analysis, companies are able to identify gaps where they are most vulnerable so they can address them quickly and efficiently.
- *Product development and innovation*: The use of data analysis in product development and innovation generates improved decision-making through objective, reliable evaluations. It creates the ability to verify product concepts and models quicker and enables companies to gain access to user feedback more efficiently. This ultimately provides companies a more comprehensive understanding of their products and services, and where there are deficiencies, while enabling them to validate the proof of concept faster.
- *Supply chain management*: By using analytics in the supply chain, companies are able to predict risks, identify gaps in their system, and quickly spot activities that are wasteful or lacking value. This leads to a more efficient business.[2]

Taking Action

In the past, you were able to just "go with your gut." This is no longer the case. You are now required to have data to back up your decisions. Though there has always been some level of data used to determine a course of action, the advanced ability to dissect information to determine how to proceed will be used more due to the increased value it can generate. Companies that choose to maintain the status quo with decision-making will not be able to keep up. Leverage the tools and programs that enable you to dissect data and analyze information. This will enable you to make better, more informed decisions.

- What type of data could you use to improve your decision-making?
- What departments would benefit most from the use of data analytics?
- How could you automate the data you currently track to free up your time to perform other duties?

---

3. THE INTERNET OF THINGS

At its essence, the *Internet of Things* (IoT) involves technology being embedded in devices so that the ability to send and receive data is feasible. This connectivity enables companies to track the physical location of everyday objects. IoT increases the speed of business decisions, and eliminates unnecessary, manual involvement.

In 1990, the world had roughly 300,000 connected devices. In 2013, there were 9 billion. In 2025, there are expected to be an estimated 1 trillion devices with this technology. Areas where IoT will be valuable include ordering more resources when supplies are low, tracking the location of a customer's order, and monitoring the process flow of production. All of these activities can already be accomplished, but incorporation of IoT enables them to be completed without manual intervention.

This will be valuable in many ways. For example, when a store is running low on a certain product, employees won't need to go into the system to manually place an order. Instead, when a predetermined threshold is reached, IoT will cause that product to be ordered automatically. This will ensure employees are not interrupted. Instead, they will be able to continue performing their work. Bringing this to a more granular level, when you run low on paper towels at home, IoT will create an order at Amazon, Walmart, or other retail company, and have that product shipped directly to you.[3]

Taking Action

IoT has extraordinary potential, especially in regard to the speed at which your business will be able to operate. To ensure you produce optimal value, you must determine the best approach for using it.

- How is your industry using IoT?
- What are the devices and objects in which technology can be imbedded in so your business can speed up production?
- Where could IoT generate the most value in your business?

4. APPS AND MOBILE DEVICES

If you haven't switched everything you can over to digital/virtual yet, you've already lost. Building a virtual presence over the past two decades has been instrumental in survival. You must build on this by extending beyond just having a digital footprint; today, everything must be mobile and voice activated.

Apps and mobile devices allow people to control their lives more than ever, with every part of daily activity being affected. From controlling the temperature in the living room and monitoring sleep patterns to watching the most recent episode of your favorite television show and remote healthcare diagnosis, mobile technology and advances with apps are now demanded from the marketplace.

Mobile connectivity will not stop there. Over the course of the next decade, customers will become increasingly interested in wearable devices. More than just a watch that will enable you to read email, text with friends, or track how many steps you take, wearables being developed will have far more functionality. Watches will tell you which friends are in close proximity, glasses will alert you to stores in your area that are having a sale, and earrings will play music for you depending on your mood.

The use of voice-activated products will also skyrocket over the next decade. Companies like Amazon, Google, and Apple (among others) have created advanced, voice-activated technology that is revolutionizing consumer behavior. This paradigm shift empowers people to simplify their lives by enabling them to communicate with a device directly, rather than through the use of a keyboard.

Taking Action

If you delay adopting apps and mobile devices similar to the way many companies delayed embracing websites and social media, you will lose. The world has never been more mobile, so the idea that you can avoid incorporating this advance is false. Instead, you must meet this challenge head-on.

- What have you done to embrace the transition into mobile?
- What app or mobile device could you create that would enable you to communicate with your consumers more directly (and effectively)?
- How will voice technology disrupt your industry? And how can you include it in your business?

---

5. MONEY MANAGEMENT

The way we exchange money has consistently changed over the years. Businesses (and people) used to pay with cash, then navigated to checks, then credits, and then finally to transferring funds from bank to bank. Each of these advances resulted in a quicker exchange of money. The notion that it will stop there is inaccurate.

Advances in technology are enabling the ability to exchange funds quicker and easier. Two examples are Mobile Payment Systems and Blockchain.

Mobile Payment Systems allow money to be transferred from business to business, business to consumer, and person to person quickly and efficiently. This has taken shape through various mobile apps and has gained traction, especially with younger generations. Rather than carrying around cash or credit cards, people transfer money on their phone using an app. This trend will continue to grow as new generations join the workforce.

Similarly, Blockchain allows companies to forgo government involvement of financial transactions through the use of bitcoin and other cryptocurrencies. Through the digital exchange of finances, companies can avoid transfer of government-backed funds. This eliminates a step in a customary business transaction, causing the process to be faster, cheaper, and more efficient. Through the billions of transactions that occur every day, the elimination of this single step, multiplied out will have enormous implications worldwide.

Taking Action

Streamlining the exchange of funds between you and your customers cannot be overstated. If you want to be competitive, you must find ways to update the way you pay suppliers and bill customers, including through the use of mobile apps and cryptocurrencies.

- How have mobile apps or cryptocurrencies disrupted your industry?
- When was the last time your company assessed how it billed customers or paid suppliers? What could you change to make this process faster/more efficient?
- How has your competition changed the way it bills customers?

6. EXPANDED HOME DELIVERY

The days of buying potato chips, toothpaste, and aspirin at the local convenience store are coming to an end. Though there will inevitably be products that consumers are more comfortable purchasing in person, the overwhelming majority of household goods will be bought online. Streamlined service through purchases on the web will provide customers the opportunity to remove unnecessary trips to the grocery store.

This is already taking place through Amazon Prime, UberEats, Grubhub, Shipt, and Instacart, to name a few, and displays no sign of slowing down. Instead, this multibillion-dollar industry will continue to grow while simultaneously changing the way we look at home delivery.

Most notably, the speed and efficiency that will take place will be especially disruptive. In the past, overnight delivery was seen as exceptional, but today, companies are able to deliver an entire car filled with groceries in under 2 hours. Combining this with automation, it won't be surprising to experience a driverless Uber pulling up to your house to deliver a four-course meal that has already been cooked less than an hour after you press a single button on your phone.

This is an amazing opportunity for delivery companies and a huge benefit for consumers. However, it will be catastrophic for convenience stores and small shops. Stores that rely on consistent revenue from a constant stream of loyal consumers will inevitably fade away.

Similarly, expedited delivery will cause challenges for big chains as well. High costs for large brick and mortar facilities (i.e. grocery stores) will not be necessary because of the ability for companies to ship household goods and perishable items directly to the consumer. Strategically placed fulfillment centers will be able to deliver straight to the customer, removing a cumbersome and costly step in the value chain. This will make considerable waves across the industry.

Taking Action

If you sell household goods and have yet to leverage home delivery, you are behind. Consumers demand streamlined service. In order to keep up, you must develop a way to get your product into your customers' hands with as little disruption to their lives as possible.

- What products can you deliver to your customers?
- What company can you partner with to deliver your products to your customers?
- How can you compete with industry leaders who are already delivering goods?

7. THE DEATH OF TELEVISION ADVERTISING

In 2019, companies spent over $70 billion on television ads. This is all in direct contrast to the universal response everyone has when a commercial comes on; people instinctively either pull out their smartphone or change the channel. Their focus is far from the commercials that are supposed to entice us into buying new products and services.[4]

Technology has transformed consumer behavior. Just a short time ago, if you would have said that television ads would lack relevance, no one would have believed you. Yet due to the digital takeover, this is true. Television ads have never been less relevant than now.

Broad approaches toward attracting customers used to work, but this is no longer the case. The internet offers a dynamic alternative that is far more intriguing. Based on search history, algorithms, and the power of distinct habits, companies are able to target potential customers with amazing accuracy. This shift will continue over the next 10 years, with commercials continuing to become less relevant.

Taking Action

The Superbowl is the only television show in which people choose to watch commercials. During every other program, consumers are not paying attention. You need to eliminate the notion that TV commercials have relevance and begin pouring your money into internet and social media marketing.

- Over the past 5 years, what is the ROI in your television advertising? Internet and social media?
- What investments have you made in internet and social media marketing?
- What social media platforms can you use to reach your target audience?

---

8. THE GIG ECONOMY

Forget employees jumping from job to job, the trend that is growing the most is the Gig Economy. Rather than being tied down to a specific company or particular role, independent workers are contracting with organizations for short-term engagements. Popular sites like Fiverr, Upwork, and Freelancer are all sophisticated platforms that bring individuals looking for temporary work and companies that have a certain task to be completed together in a safe environment. Services on these sites range from website design and teaching a foreign language to janitorial services and providing tennis lessons.

The Gig Economy has many benefits. Workers are able to take on projects that are appealing to them and a good fit for their skillset, schedule, and budget. With many employees (especially employees new to the workplace) valuing their freedom over a steady paycheck, people who are not tied down to a specific job or schedule are able to have more control over their lives.

Similarly, companies are able to be more fiscally sound through the use of temporary workers. By avoiding big salaries and expensive benefits, companies can afford to bring on new talent for projects without making a big investment. Rather than having to worry about adding new employees that will inevitably weigh the company down, the use of temporary workers enables them to be nimble, while only investing in the talent they need at that time. This also broadens the talent pool, improving the value the organization can deliver to customers.

It is evident there are numerous dynamics that make the Gig Economy unattractive for some people and companies, but the use of this strategy will continue to grow due to the flexibility, cost structure, and changing needs people and businesses have.

Taking Action

With people becoming increasingly interested in having an opportunity to experience various roles and functions, and companies always looking for ways to cut costs and expand their talent pool, the Gig Economy is a perfect marriage for many people and businesses. Becoming more open to this concept and how you could potentially address certain projects could enable you to be more fluid with your hiring practices.

- Where can you cut costs by using short-term freelancers instead of permanent employees?
- What projects could you use temporary employees for?
- What skills are lacking in your organization that could be filled by freelance workers?

9. RESKILLING THE WORKFORCE

Education has never been easier to access for more people than it is today. Online learning is revolutionizing the way students get an education, while building a stronger, more skilled workforce. This has transformed the workplace. Many roles that were once highly coveted are now saturated with talent. Alternatively, jobs that used to be undesirable or lacking an opportunity for considerable growth are now great paths.

Because of this, the role of universities, trade schools, and technical programs are transforming. No longer are people focused exclusively on earning a degree so they can check a box on a job application. Instead, they are placing emphasis on acquiring a unique set of skills that will prepare them for a specific career. Because, while getting a degree in leisure studies or general education could have been valuable previously, their importance now pales in comparison to unique skills like coding, web design, and analytics. To succeed, you must have a distinct talent that will bring value to an organization.

Further, the existing workforce lacks the skills necessary to use all of the new technologies that are entering into the business ecosystem. This requires them to get additional education. This reskilling, combined with online learning, makes it clear that there will be an extraordinary push toward gaining coveted new talents, skills, and abilities, causing many people to invest in more education.

Taking Action

Regardless of how old you are and what you do, if you believe you do not need to develop your skills and expand your talents, you are wrong. The workplace has changed more in the past 10 years than it did in the previous 50. So, the notion that you can rely on what you learned yesterday is inaccurate. You must invest in your future to be successful, regardless of your age.

From a company's perspective, the importance of ensuring your employees have the tools necessary to perform their role in the changing environment is also important. You must identify how your industry and market are evolving.

- How has your industry and market changed in the past 10 years?
- Where are your industry and market moving toward that will require employees to develop new skills?
- What can you do to be sure you and your workforce have the necessary skills to succeed in the future?

10. FUNCTIONALITY OVER FORMALITY

Formalities have long been drivers of workplace environments, quite often, at the expense of productivity. While companies would change to meet the needs of employees, it wouldn't come without a price or extensive analysis. Over the course of the next decade, this will change considerably. With the transformation of the business ecosystem and increased competitive nature of every industry and market, the importance of rethinking how to optimize productivity is critical. Specifically:

- *Workplaces will look different than in the past*: Open floor plans, desk sharing, and collaboration zones will foster creativity and growth. Businesses will also develop office furniture that will generate a more comfortable atmosphere in which employees can be at their best. From standing desks and treadmill workstations to contemporary couches and quiet rooms, the traditional office look will fade away. In its place will be environments that are conducive to getting the best out of employees.
- *Middlemen will disappear*: In the past, connectivity happened through brokers who were able to connect one person or company with another. In today's economy, the internet is the middleman, making the broker unnecessary. This is already taking place in numerous industries. For example, travel agents used to ensure that you would get the best deal when going on a vacation. Today, families will peruse numerous vacation sites rather than paying for an agent.
- *Diverse/matrix teams will increase exponentially*: The days of simple problem solving that involve a single business unit or department are gone. In its place are challenges that extend beyond a single team. This requires employees to have strong interpersonal skills that enable them to collaborate with different departments in the organization to solve complex problems.
- *Results-oriented work environment*: As long as you are producing value, it won't matter where you do your work or how long it takes you to complete. Employees, whether in the office or working remotely, will be responsible for completing a core set of tasks, and they will be evaluated specifically against these duties, not on how many hours they are logging. This change in perspective will enable employees to focus solely on being productive, instead of how much time they put in.

Taking Action

In the past, having a structured organization with firmly established rules and regulations was paramount to success. Rules and regulations are still important, but priorities have shifted, and policies have become more liberal. In today's environment, you must focus on optimizing your workplace at any cost, and this means changing the way your business functions.

- Where are you placing formality over functionality?
- What change could you make that would increase engagement and not reduce productivity (i.e. employees working remotely, removing excessive policies, eliminating business silos, etc.)?
- What policy have you put off changing because you do not want to rock the boat?

BRINGING IT ALL TOGETHER

These are not the only changes that will take place over the next 10 years. However, they are changes that will affect every industry and market in the world. This requires you to identify how you can implement these changes to successfully improve your organization.

Take heed, if you do not take this seriously, you will be left behind. Conversely, by leveraging these changes, you will be able to capitalize on new opportunities to generate increased value, simplify operations, and maximize profits. Determine how you can take advantage of these changes to take your company to the next level and then execute.

NOTES

1. Chea, Catherine. "7 Industries That Will Be Taken Over by AI and Robots." *Datafloq.com.* https://datafloq.com/read/7-industries-taken-over-ai-robots/4128 (accessed April 14, 2020).
2. Kopanakis, John. "5 Real-World Examples of How Brands Are Using Big Data Analytics." *Mentionlytics.com.* www.mentionlytics.com/blog/5-real-world-examples-of-how-brands-are-using-big-data-analytics/ (accessed April 14, 2020).
3. Analytics Vidhya. "10 Real World Applications of Internet of Things (IoT) – Explained in Videos." *Analyticsvidhya.com.* www.analyticsvidhya.com/blog/2016/08/10-youtube-videos-explaining-the-real-world-applications-of-internet-of-things-iot/ (accessed April 14, 2020).
4. Poggi, Jeanine. "TV Ad Spend to Drop 3 Percent to $70.3 Billion in 2019: Report." *Adage.com.* https://adage.com/article/media/tv-ad-spend-drop-3-percent-703-billion-2019-report/2214661 (accessed April 15, 2020).

Conclusion

What do you do?

What could make you obsolete or replaceable?

What change can you make to eliminate this risk?

What specific actions can you take to execute this change?

In the end, these four core questions are all that matter. They are a gateway to sustained success and provide a structured path to delivering value to the market. Changes in the business world will never stop; it is how you manage them that will either drive you toward success or cripple your business.

Digging deeper, in today's economic climate, changes are coming faster, are more intense, and have greater consequences than ever before. If you become stagnant, you will become irrelevant. If you remain comfortable, you will be unnecessary. If you maintain the status quo, you will die. Whether you want to believe this or not, this is the reality of the situation. Because of this, in order to have sustained success, you must determine the actions you need to take to transform your business.

Looking back over the past 10 years, how quickly have industries and markets changed? How much have these changes either catapulted or destroyed the value of companies? How much has the willingness or resistance to change affected the success of organizations?

And most importantly, how much will the willingness or resistance to change affect your business moving forward?

Technology, processes, and people will always continue to advance and improve. This requires you to do the same. You cannot afford to keep business as usual, be indecisive, or remain passive. If you want to succeed, you must change and execute. You must meet the demands of the market head-on, while relentlessly looking to optimize productivity.

Change and Execute will enable you to do this. This book was written to help you transform your business by providing specific guidance and direction focused on improving productivity and generating sustained success. The power to transform your business is in your hands. Use this book to change and execute and take your organization to the next level!

Appendix: Companies and Industries That Failed to Change

Below is a list of companies and industries referenced in the book that have died, gone bankrupt, or experienced extraordinary loss because they did not change to meet the demands of the new economy. Sadly, this list is only a small percentage of companies and industries that have experienced devastating consequences because of the inability to change.

A&P
AOL
Bealls
Best Buy
Blackberry
Blockbuster
Borders Bookstore
Circuit City
Classmates.com
CompUSA
Friendster
Gander Mountain
General Electric
Goody's
Gordmans
Hardware Stores
Hotel Chains
Independent Bookstores
J.Crew
JCPenney
Music Shops
Myspace
Neiman Marcus
Palais Royal
Payless Shoes
Peebles
Radio Shack
Sears
Sports Authority
Stage Stores
Taxi Companies
TiVo
Tower Records
Toys "R" Us
Vintage Furniture Shops
Xerox
Yahoo!

Index

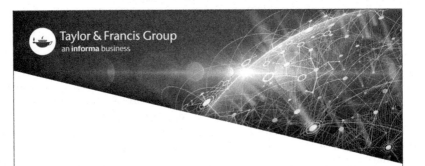

Taylor & Francis eBooks

www.taylorfrancis.com

A single destination for eBooks from Taylor & Francis
with increased functionality and an improved user
experience to meet the needs of our customers.

90,000+ eBooks of award-winning academic content in
Humanities, Social Science, Science, Technology, Engineering,
and Medical written by a global network of editors and authors.

TAYLOR & FRANCIS EBOOKS OFFERS:

A streamlined
experience for
our library
customers

A single point
of discovery
for all of our
eBook content

Improved
search and
discovery of
content at both
book and
chapter level

REQUEST A FREE TRIAL
support@taylorfrancis.com

Printed in the United States
By Bookmasters